Impact:
WORKING WITH
SEXUAL ABUSERS

Edited by
Stacey Bird Edmunds

Impact: Working with Sexual Abusers

Editor: Stacey Bird Edmunds

Production Editors: Euan Bear and Eileen Murray

ISBN: 1-884444-42-3

Order From:
Safer Society Press
P.O. Box 340
Brandon, Vermont 05733-0340
(802) 247-3132

Contents

Introduction:
A Personal and Professional
Perspective on Burnout

In 1978 when I first began treating sexually abusive patients at the North Florida Evaluation and Treatment Center in Gainesville, Florida, I had little understanding of the type of work I was entering. It was my second job after graduate school and the description seemed interesting. I had no previous training or education about treating sexual abusers. My only information was that the forensic patients I would be treating were convicted sexual offenders, and they were considered dangerous.

I knew nothing about sexual abusers as a clinical population and knew very little about sexual abuse. When I began working in this field, I believed most of the myths then held by our society regarding sexual abuse, sex offenders, and the victims of sexual abuse. In 1978 people were barely talking about rape, and child molestation was seldom in the media.

As I enter my twentieth year of treating sexual abusers, I can look back and assess the impact this work has had on my life both personally and professionally. I was unable to do this honestly until about eight years ago. On a personal level, I found that many areas of my life were affected. I experienced difficulty trusting people I met. Almost every time I saw a man walking toward a child at the mall I glared, suspecting him of being a sexual abuser, while at the same time, I wanted to support fathers to be more involved with their children in healthy ways. There is no doubt in my mind that I look at the world through a very different set of glasses than my family, friends, and others who do not work with sexual abuse. One of my colleagues calls this skewed perception "being bent." It felt like the loss of innocence. There were few, if any "safe" places or people left in the world.

I experienced a heightened awareness of being a male in our society. I became supersensitive in all my interactions with women. I felt a kind of gender shame, because so many of my sexually abusive clients were men. For some periods I was very close to rage nearly all the time, and I criticized friends for not exercising what I considered "enough" supervision over their children. In the first five years of working with sex offenders, I was very uncomfortable holding my infant niece, and I flat out refused to have anything to do with bathing or diapering. But, on a more hopeful note, now that I have two small children in my household, I can bathe and diaper them without work-generated qualms.

When working in the phallometric assessment lab, listening to deviant fantasy after deviant fantasy, I had no fantasy life and little sex life. Later on, that was reversed as I became desensitized to the identities of participants and victims and experienced a higher than usual sex drive. I also began questioning my past dating behavior during adolescence, worried that some of it might now be considered sexual harassment or abuse.

I wish there had been more open discussion of these issues when I was most actively struggling with them. I would have availed myself of the opportunity if any of the programs I was associated with had had the resources, foresight, and culture of staff support to provide a constructive forum for such discussions. As a program director, I found myself encouraging staff to debrief their experiences, but I held back my issues, feeling I should not reveal that part of my life to my employees.

Finally, as a result of conducting my personal inventory, I found myself able to achieve the necessary balance to continue work in this field. I'm not saying that the impact issues have all gone away, they have not. However, I am finding ways to take appropriate responsibility without going overboard. I believe I am better equipped to disengage the adrenaline response of suspecting or charging abuse when it is not warranted. I have established appropriate boundaries at work and at home, and I take the necessary steps to maintain them. I have learned to practice what I preach, and I like most people, realize that my work responsibilities are to do the best I can with what I've got. In addition I try to keep in mind that each client successfully treated may save anywhere from one to several hundred adults and children from being sexually victimized.

I know many sexual abuse treatment professionals have not conducted this type of personal inventory. Although in my travels around the country lecturing and consulting I see a growing number of practitioners beginning to deal with these issues, many professionals still struggle with the impact of their work on their personal and professional lives. This is why I believe this book is so very important and timely.

At the same time, there have been many rewarding moments in my work, providing much personal satisfaction. I have seen families resolve sexual abuse and reunite in a healthy lifestyle because of treatment. I have seen abusers turn their lives around and become productive citizens and members of their communities. Through the years I have witnessed a growing number of bright, young, capable people enter the field and grow professionally. I have had the opportunity to travel all over my country and in five foreign countries because of my involvement in treating sexual abusers.

During my career I have met some of the nicest, kindest, and most intelligent people anyone could have the privilege to know. I have felt personal satisfaction with my work and accomplishments. I believe I have made a significant contribution to the field of sexual abuse prevention and treatment and positively influenced and affected others who do this most important work. All of this feels good.

I have worked in a variety of settings, including prisons, state hospitals, community mental health programs, private clinics, and youth programs. My work has brought me into contact more than 5,000 children, adolescents, and adults who have engaged in sexually abusive behaviors. These clients and patients have been as old as eighty, as young as five, male and female, Hispanic, Caucasian, African-American, Native American, and of still other cultures and races. My work has broadened my experience and enriched my life in numerous ways.

On the other hand, I know that my career has affected me professionally in ways that are harmful and personally challenging. What do I do with my sense of rage and helplessness at witnessing the horrors of our criminal justice system? How can we cope when our prisoner clients are raped, beaten and assaulted, when they commit suicide, or as happened to one of my clients, when they are murdered?

It has also been painful to witness the impact of this work on my colleagues and friends. What could I do with my anger and grief when one of the staff members in a program I directed was murdered by a client, when another committed suicide after being raped in her home? Hearing that several colleagues have been attacked by a patient or client, how can I maintain a sense of personal safety? This work has at times made me question daily my own safety and that of my staff and my family.

I have been shunned by other mental health professionals for working with sexual abusers, as have my friends and colleagues. I and my friends and colleagues have been battered with words by the media and the public who often refuse to find any meaning in the work we do. On one radio talk show I was told by a caller, "If you are treating these people and find any value in them, then you must be a sex offender yourself."

Like my colleagues I have heard the countless descriptions of the sexually abusive acts my clients have perpetrated on helpless victims. I have also heard their personal stories of child abuse, neglect, and experienced their pain in addition to the pain of their victims. I have watched their personal struggles through treatment and the struggles of their families, spouses, and significant others who have decided to support them in treatment.

I have experienced the joys of treatment successes and the frustration and self-blame of treatment failures. All of us who treat sexual abusers have clients who have reoffended. We often take responsibility for these clients and feel as though we are on some level responsible for that next victim being sexually abused. These and many other issues contribute to the potential burnout all of us face in working in the field of sexual abuse, and specifically with sexually abusive clients.

Two years ago, and independent of other researchers, Stacey Bird Edmunds, then a staff member of the Safer Society Foundation, and I developed a questionnaire on impact issues related to working with sexual abusers. We distributed it at the Association for the Treatment of Sexual Abusers' (ATSA) Thirteenth Annual Research and Treatment Conference held in San Francisco. As a result of conducting this survey, other professionals doing similar research and work talked to us. Some of their research and ideas are now a part of this book. The results of that survey are in Chapter One of this book. Additional chapters by invited authors address the various aspects of impact in working with sexual abuse and some ways we as professionals can work toward taking care of ourselves.

On November 24, 1996, I attended a two-and-a-half-day National Summit convened by the United States Department of Justice, Office of Justice Programs.[1] During a roundtable discussion titled "Care for the Care Givers," impact and burnout issues were addressed. First, we noted that few programs treating sexual abusers have built into the workplace mechanisms that address the impact of this work on staff. Some participants noted that it is difficult to institutionalize meetings designed for staff self-care. Heavy caseloads, limited resources, and coordination of meeting times make it difficult to pull staff together for this purpose.

In addition the group noted a tremendous fear of self-disclosure in staff meetings. Many treatment providers are concerned that disclosure of some impact issues might result in dismissal, reassignment, or loss of promotions and job opportunities. In some cases, participants felt that such disclosures would result in their professionalism being questioned, and that supervisors would respond accordingly.

Environmental factors were considered as having the potential to compound the problem, especially for state-run institutions such as prisons and state hospitals. Prisons are one of the most negative environments in which we may work. Few prison administrators and staff support offender treatment programs, though they may exist within the institution. Chronic understaffing at state mental hospitals heightens workplace stress. In these two situations, and in any private ones that resemble them, staff burnout increases when negative aspects of the work and the environment take up energy that could be focused on the positive aspects of this work and the rewards of helping people turn their lives around.

Also discussed was the issue of whether programs should require that staff attend a regular meeting designed to help them deal with impact issues. The roundtable participants agreed that mandating attendance at such meetings might ultimately prove more harmful than helpful. Thus, the question arises about what programs should do to help staff members and reduce some of the impact of working in the sexual abuser treatment field. I would like to offer three suggestions.

---

[1] A National Summit: Promoting Public Safety Through the Effective Management of Sex Offenders in the Community. Washington, D.C. November 24–26, 1996.

First, I believe that as a profession, we need to seriously consider dealing with staff impact and burnout before we even hire a candidate for any offender-contact position. I believe we have an obligation to inform persons we interview to work in this field of the potential impact this work may have on their lives. We should give prospective employees the opportunity to understand the nature of the work and adequate time to decide whether they are prepared to deal with the potential impact. Unlike candidates for other helping professions such as police, rescue, and medical services, who are likely to have some understanding of the impact and burnout issues, most professionals entering the sexual abuser treatment field have little understanding of the nature of the clientele or the potential impact this work may have on their lives.

Second, we should require that everyone we hire to work in the sexual abuser treatment field must attend an initial orientation and training session that not only teaches them about the work, but also addresses the potential personal impact of working with sexual abusers.

Third, while programs should not mandate staff meetings to specifically address impact issues, we should require as a condition of accreditation or as a standard of operation that programs offer an open forum for staff to attend who do want to talk about the personal impact of working with sexual abusers. Such programs must be structured to keep staff impact disclosures confidential and to support staff in their professional growth rather than to punish disclosure of spill-over effects.

It is for the reasons and issues noted above that the Safer Society Press has decided to publish this book. We consider it an evolving document. As we discover more research and writings in this area, we hope to add future materials. Therefore, if you or your colleagues are researching or writing about impact and/or burnout in working with sexual abuse, we invite you to call the Safer Society regarding the inclusion of your work to future editions of this book. The Safer Society Foundation thanks you for your support and wishes you continued success in your work.

Robert E. Freeman-Longo, MRC, LPC, CCJS
Director, The Safer Society Press
Brandon, Vermont

I

The Personal Impact of Working With Sex Offenders

STACEY BIRD EDMUNDS, M.S. Candidate[1]

Research that examines the personal impact of providing treatment to victims and perpetrators of sexual abuse disproportionately focuses on the victim-therapist (Allen & Brekke, 1995; Bloom, 1993; Briere, 1992; Grosch & Olsen, 1994; McCann & Pearlman, 1990, 1993; Oliveri & Waterman, 1993). Despite the need for exploration, few studies examine the impact on clinicians of providing therapy to the perpetrators of sexual abuse. Although several nonempirical reports have concluded that job-related stress, or burnout, is relational to providing therapy to such abusers, only one published study was found to document the hypothesized coexistence (Farrenkopf, 1992).

Researchers believe that stress is inherent in many occupations. A study conducted by the Northwestern National Life Insurance Company concludes that 53% of all supervisors and 34% of all nonsupervisors consider their jobs to be highly stressful (Custer, 1994). Jack Wiggins, president of the Psychological Development Center in Cleveland, Ohio, and past president of the American Psychological Association, reports that 35% of all workers experience job-related stress to the extent that they have a diagnosable mental condition (Custer, 1994). These statistics should be carefully considered. How might job stress negatively affect the health and well-being of employees? How might the health and well-being of workers affect work performance, interpersonal relationships, and appropriate functioning in society? The possible effects of this trickle-down process seem endless. Consequently, researchers must augment the evaluation of job-related stress to include occupations that they have, until now, frequently ignored.

Individuals such as mental health workers, whose profession requires continuous contact with other people, are particularly prone to burnout. Exacerbating that susceptibility is the assumption of responsibility that is intrinsic in therapeutic

[1] At the time this survey was coducted, Stacey Bird Edmunds was a staff member of The Safer Society Foundation, Brandon, Vermont, 05733.

relationships (Kottler, 1993; Peaslee, 1995; Skorupa & Agresti, 1993; Sullivan, 1993). For clinicians providing therapy to sex abusers, the assumption of responsibility extends not only to the client but to the victims, potential victims, and society. The sex-abuser treatment provider has the demanding clinical task to rehabilitate the offender and a self-imposed obligation to safeguard others' welfare. Perhaps due to such responsibility, Scott (1989) declares psychotherapy with criminals to be "the most demanding task in the entire arena of mental health" (p. 225).

Ostensibly unique to the role of the sexual-abuser treatment provider is the need to repeatedly address and evaluate the disturbing thoughts and behaviors of sexually abusive people. Clinicians frequently accept the prevention of further victimization as the primary goal of sex-offender treatment, and consequently, they must review the dynamics of past offenses. Details of violent fantasies and horrifying interpersonal sex crimes are a familiar focus of the therapeutic sessions. Despite recognizing control, not comprehension, as the primary treatment goal, treatment providers must nevertheless privately process the emotion-evoking information (Peaslee, 1995). As a result, sex-abuse therapists inevitably experience strong emotional and cognitive responses to offending behavior (Kearns, 1995). Although this focus is only one of the many potential stress-inducing elements of the job, the repeated confrontation of these issues can be a considerable factor in therapist burnout.

Researchers define burnout in different ways. Freudenberger (1975), believed to be the originator of the term, described the condition as "failing, wearing out, or becoming exhausted through excessive demands on energy, strength, or resources" (quoted in Ackerley, Burnell, Holder, & Kurdek, 1988, p. 624). Pines and Maslach (1978) described burnout as "a syndrome of physical and emotional exhaustion" (p. 233). Other theorists have concluded that burnout is the experience of fatigue and frustration in response to unsatisfied expectations (Yiu-kee & Tang, 1995). Despite the variability in definition, studies that have focused on burnout have consistently examined several comparable emotional, psychological, and physical factors (Ackerley et al, 1988; Farrenkopf, 1993; Maslach & Jackson, 1986; McCann & Pearlman, 1990; Pines & Maslach, 1978; Yiu-kee & Tang, 1995).

Over the past two decades, considerable research has examined burnout as experienced by the mental health worker (Ackerley et al, 1988; Pines & Maslach, 1978; Raquepaw & Miller, 1989; Skorupa & Agresti, 1993; Sullivan, 1993; Yiu-kee & Tang, 1995). The literature presents several factors associated with burnout, including, but not limited to: age, gender, work conditions, isolation, over-involvement with work, ambiguity about one's employment role, years in the field, hours per work week, hours spent with difficult clients, and supervision (Ackerley et al, 1988; Farrenkopf, 1993; Maslach & Jackson, 1982; Savicki & Cooley, 1987; Yiu-kee & Tang, 1995). These factors are often further classified by their assignment to three descriptive categories developed by Maslach & Jackson (1982, 1984): organizational factors, interpersonal factors, and personal factors. Some researchers, however, have applied modified descriptive groupings. Ackerley et al. (1988) designated five categories to organize the correlates of burnout: 1) demographic factors; 2) objective work characteristics; 3) types of therapeutic activities; 4) types of issues faced during work; and 5) factors in the therapeutic setting. Despite the variations of classification, a common thread remains. Treatment providers often recognize the negative personal effects of burnout as related to their working conditions or personal characteristics.

Researchers have identified several personal characteristics and employment conditions as risk factors of burnout. Pines, Aronson, and Kafry (1981) directly relate burnout to the continuous or repeated emotional pressure of intense involvement with people over an extended period. Long work hours, severity of a client's problems, and incongruity between a therapist's expectations and a client's growth also may increase the likelihood of burnout (Kestnbaum, 1984; Pines & Maslach, 1978). Additional factors include many client-contact hours, many 'difficult' clients in a caseload, and inadequate access to preparatory professional training and support groups (Bernard, Fuller, Robbins & Shaw, 1989; Farber, 1983).

Previous research has also identified various symptoms of burnout. Increases in fatigue, disturbed sleep patterns, insensitivity to others, absenteeism, frustration, cynicism, and depression represent a partial list. Conversely, decreased levels of self-esteem, anger management, leisure time, sex drive, confidence in personal safety, and positive thoughts or feelings regarding the future are similarly recognized as symptoms of burnout (Edelwich & Brodsky, 1980; Freeman-Longo, 1993; Pines, et al., 1981; Pines & Maslach, 1978; Raquepaw & Miller, 1989; Taylor-Brown, Johnson, Hunter & Rockowitz, 1981).

The purpose of this study was to collect descriptive data for a sample of sex-abuser treatment professionals and to develop a profile of personal characteristics, employment conditions, and burnout symptoms. Despite the acknowledged lack of scientific controls, the study has been useful in obtaining valuable information from professionals working with perpetrators of sexual abuse. As previously noted, therapists need additional research to fully recognize the personal effects of providing treatment to sex abusers.

Method

Respondents

A convenience sample of sex-abuser treatment providers was obtained at the thirteenth annual national treatment and research conference of the Association for the Treatment of Sexual Abusers (ATSA). Of the 636 Personal Impact Surveys provided, 289 were returned. Of those returned, 13 incomplete surveys were discarded. Participation was anonymous and strictly voluntary. Respondents included 130 female (47%) and 146 male (53%) sex-abuser treatment professionals, most of whom were between the ages of 36 and 45 (61%). The respondents' primary occupations ranged from therapists (60%), to administrative staff (25%), probation or parole specialists (6%), direct-care providers (5%), and case managers (3%). Five respondents (2%) either specified occupations not listed on the survey form or failed to respond. The majority of participants (48%) had fifteen or more years of experience working in the mental health field, but only 16% had spent those years working with sex abusers (See Figure 1). Most respondents had worked with sex abusers between 3 and 8 years (47%). Of those responding to the Personal Impact Survey, 53% held a master's degree, and 26% possessed doctorate degrees. Most (66%) respondents worked an average of 41 or more hours a week, and the average work-day was between 7 and 9 hours (53%). Ninety-eight respondents (36%) accounted for 11 to 20 hours of their work week as direct client

FIGURE 1
PARTICIPANT DEMOGRAPHICS

Primary Occupation:		*Primary Work Setting:*	
Therapist	60%	Private Practice	29%
Probation/Parole	6%	Residential / Hospital	20%
Direct Care	5%	Day Treatment	1%
Case Manager	3%	Prison Based	22%
Administration	25%	Community / M.H.	16%
Other / No Response	2%	Other / No Response	12%

Years in Mental Health Field		*Years Working with Sexual Abusers*	
0-2 years	5%	0-2 years	14%
3-5 years	11%	3-5 years	23%
6-8 years	11%	6-8 years	24%
9-11 years	13%	9-11 years	14%
12-14 years	11%	12-14 years	8%
15 or more years	48%	15 or more years	16%

Highest Degree Obtained		*Average Work Day*	
Doctorate	26	0-3 hours	1%
Masters	53%	4-6 hours	5%
Bachelor	13%	7-9 hours	53%
Associate	2%	10-12 hours	38%
High School	2%	13 or more hours	4%
Other / No Response	8%		

Average Work Week		*Hours per week with Sexual Abusers*	
1-8 hours	0	Zero hours	2%
9-16 hours	1%	1-10 hours	28%
17-24 hours	3%	11-20 hours	36%
25-32 hours	1%	21-30 hours	14%
33-40 hours	29%	31-40 hours	11%
41 or more hours	66%	41 or more hours	9%

time, and 28% reported 1 hour to 10 hours per week spent in direct contact with sex abusers (see Figure 1).

Concerning sex-abuser clienteles, 89% of the treatment professionals said that 91% to 100% of their workload comprised male abusers. Of this male clientele, 41% were between the ages of 10 and 20 years, and 41% were between the ages of 31 and 40 years. Forty percent (40%) of the respondents were working with female abusers; 38% of those respondents cataloged those clients as 1% to 15% of their caseload. Of the reported female sex-abuser clientele, 38% were between the ages of 21 and 30 years, and female clients between the ages of 10 and 20 years comprised 34% of the total clientele.

Concerning hours of training in a calendar year, 22% of the respondents claimed to spend 21 to 30 hours in training specific to working with sex abusers. Results suggest, however, that additional training is possible for many respondents as 31% quantified their yearly training as 31 to 50 hours. In addition, 12% of respondents devote 51 or more hours per year to educational training specific to working with sex abusers.

Fifty-eight percent (58%) of all respondents were responsible for the supervision of other staff members, nearly equally males (60%) and females (56%). Similarly distributed between genders were responses about satisfaction with salary. A total of 54% of respondents believed that their wages were adequate, a statement with which 52% of the female respondents and 55% of male respondents agreed.

Answers to questions about respondents' prior victimization were particularly interesting. Fifty-six percent (56%) acknowledged that they had at some time in their lives been sexually, physically, psychologically, or otherwise victimized by another person. Although no operational definitions of the abuses were offered, 22% of respondents classified themselves as survivors of psychological abuse, 11% identified themselves as prior victims of physical abuse, and 21% answered that they had been sexually victimized. Consistent with findings in the literature, more female respondents (70%) reported prior victimization than did male respondents (42%). For all types of abuse, 46% of respondents received treatment for victimization trauma, but 28% of those completing the survey offered no response.

Of the respondents acknowledging sexual victimization, 27% were females, and 16% were males. Similarly, a survey of psychologists by Pope & Feldman-Summers (1992) reported finding histories of childhood or adolescent sexual abuse for 30% of female respondents and 13% of male respondents. As with the current Personal Impact Survey, Pope & Feldman-Summers' study offered no definitions of abuse, nor did they request detailed descriptions of the victimization. A Hilton, Jennings, Drugge, & Stephens (1995) survey of the responding clinicians' childhood sex-abuse experiences offered descriptions to classify the type of abuse. Approximately 37% (36.9%) of female respondents and 27% (27.3%) of male respondents reported at least one incident of childhood sexual abuse. Rates of sexual-abuse victimization history among clinicians reported in a study conducted by Ellerby, Gutkin, Smith & Atkinson (1993) were also slightly higher than those reported in this study. Males (21.1%) and females (21.1%) were equally represented in the group of treatment providers with a history of sexual abuse victimization. With respect to therapeutic intervention, the Personal Impact Survey study found that 71% of sex-abuse survivors, 54% female and 17% male, sought counseling from a licensed therapist.

Using their professionally acquired knowledge about what constitutes sexually deviant behavior, 45% of the respondents acknowledged having private concerns about their own past personal behavior. Of those respondents, 70% were male. That figure is consistent with findings from the Ellerby et al. (1993) study, which reported that 68.4% of male respondents questioned past sexual behavior. In this study, no operational definitions were offered for sexually deviant behavior nor were details requested regarding respondents' individual actions or concerns.

An attempt was made to identify those practitioners who, during the previous year, had knowingly experienced a stressful event unrelated to their work. Fifty-three percent (53%) of respondents provided affirmative responses, identifying the existence of possibly influential external factors in the development of burnout symptoms.

Procedure

Participants were informed of the study through announcements made on the opening day of the four-day ATSA conference. Instructions for obtaining, completing, and returning surveys were provided, as was assurance that participation was strictly voluntary and completely anonymous. Surveys were made available throughout the conference at a clearly identified display table and were also distributed by the surveyor upon request. To accommodate the participants' schedules and to ensure anonymity, a return box was also placed on the table. Returned surveys were collected once a day throughout the four-day conference.

Measurement

The Personal Impact Survey

The survey consists of 62 items and is divided into 3 sections (see Appendix A). Section 1 consists of 21 forced-choice questions requesting demographic and personal information. Questions 3, 4, 5, and 19 allow a write-in reply if the participant's response is not among the available options. Section 2 contains 19 statements concerning subjective attitudes regarding work and working environment. Available responses range across a 5-point Likert-type scale. The scale ranges from 1, "completely disagree" to 5 "completely agree," with 3 representing "neither disagree nor agree." Section 3 lists 22 physical, emotional, and psychological conditions for which changes in frequency, duration, or intensity are considered symptoms of burnout. The participants were asked to respond on a 5-

point Likert-type scale similar to the scale found in Section 2 of the survey. The response set ranges from "significantly decreased" to "significantly increased," with 3 representing "no change."

Results

Forty-five percent of respondents (45%) reported that they felt adequately trained to do their work, and 53% were explicitly clear about their professional expectations. Fifty-five percent (55%) found their work to be appropriately challenging, and most respondents (63%) were convinced that their professional opinions were valued in their workplaces. Over 80% of the respondents claimed to have derived some support from family and/or close friends for the type of work done, but only 48% of the respondents perceived the same support from their respective communities. Despite the discrepancies in perceived support from external sources, most of the respondents (85%) retained a positive attitude toward working with sex abusers and perceived themselves to be effective in their duties (97%).

The positive working attitudes reported by sex-abuser treatment professionals may have been related in part to other positive perceptions about the workplace and duties. Most of the respondents believed their primary occupations offered diversity (86%), benefited others (95%), and offered adequate supervision (52%) and ample time to perform required duties (50%). In addition, 76% of respondents reported feeling comfortable in their work spaces, and many respondents reported feeling somewhat free from physical harm (63%).

Excluding reverse items (27, 28, 29, 34, 35, 36, 39, 41), 29% of respondents reported an overall increase in emotional, physical, and psychological symptoms associated with burnout (see Appendix A, Section 3). Fifteen percent (15%) of respondents cited a decrease in symptoms, and 56% experienced no changes over the previous year. Upon the examination of individual items, increased fatigue and frustration were found to have been experienced by more than 50% of all respondents. More than one-third of the respondents reported an increase in cynicism, sleep disturbances, general irritability, and private time spent thinking about work; approximately 25% acknowledged an increase in difficulty making decisions, depression, and/or depressive episodes (see Figure 2).

Of the nine elevated burnout symptoms previously discussed, most symptoms reported were consistent for men and women respondents. The greatest discrepancies were found for increased difficulty making decisions (27% for females and 19% for males), sleep disturbances (40% females and 33% males), and time spent thinking about work (48% females and 39% males). Also consistent between genders were reported increases in absenteeism (6% females and 3% males), insensitivity toward others (13% females and 18% males), alcohol or drug use (10% females and 10% males), and feelings of helplessness (20% females, 19% males).

FIGURE 2

Changes in Personal Experiences over One Year

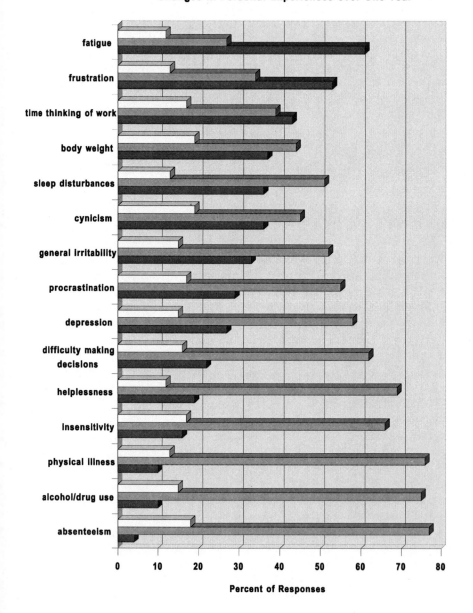

Percent of Responses

■somewhat or significantly increased ■neither increased nor decreased □somewhat or significantly decreased

The different burnout symptoms experienced by respondents identified as abuse victims and those who reported no history of abuse are interesting. Responses for six items were separated and grouped as abuse-positive responses or abuse-negative responses. Respondents self-identified as having a history of sexual, physical, psychological, or other abuse comprised 82% of those respondents reporting an increase in depression and/or depressive episodes. Similarly noteworthy was the apparently frequent representation of abuse victims among those respondents who identified an increase in frustration (61%) and cynicism (52%). A modest 13% of abuse victims were among respondents reporting increases in fatigue and sleep disturbances (see Figure 3).

Upon comparing responses of respondents reporting a history of sexual abuse and respondents denying a history of abuse, several minor and some more considerable differences were found. Sex-abuse victims noted increases in alcohol and/or drug use, insensitivity toward others, feelings of helplessness, difficulty making decisions, procrastination, depression and/or depressive episodes, and feelings of frustration (see Figure 4). They reported such experiences more often than respondents who said that they had not been abused sexually. Although these findings are not presented to establish a causal relationship, the greater frequency of reported burnout symptoms is noteworthy. Future research may offer us the ability to compare increases in burnout symptoms of abuse survivors

FIGURE 3

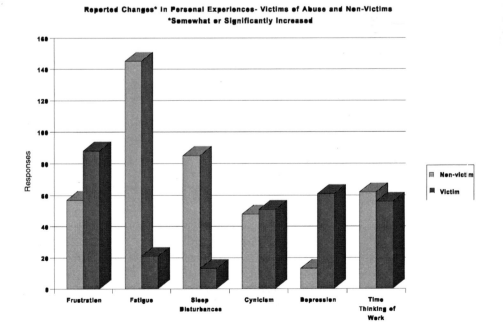

Reported Changes* in Personal Experiences- Victims of Abuse and Non-Victims
*Somewhat or Significantly Increased

FIGURE 4

Reported Changes* In Personal Experiences - Sexual Abuse Victims & Non-victims
*Somewhat or Significantly Increased

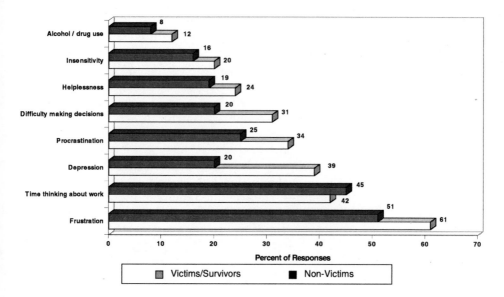

working with sex-abuse perpetrators with symptom increases for abuse survivors employed in other professions.

Before collecting survey results, it appeared reasonable to assume that a greater degree of change in burnout symptoms would occur for professionals spending the most hours per week in direct client-contact. It was assumed that a greater disparity in increased burnout symptoms would exist between professionals working the most client-contact hours per week and practitioners working the least number of client-contact hours. This hypothesis was not supported by the findings: respondents reporting the greatest increases in cynicism (43%), frustration (62%), and fatigue (67%) worked an average of 11 to 20 client-contact hours per week (see Figures 5a-5c).

For reversed items in Section 3, respondents reported decreases in leisure time spent with friends (43%), self-esteem (12%), ability to control anger (13%), confidence in personal safety (19%), and positive thoughts toward the future (20%). Although responses were largely similar for both genders, 25% of the female participants reported experiencing less confidence in personal safety, but only 13% of male participants responded that they felt increasingly unsafe.

Fifty-four percent of respondents (54%) reported no changes in their sex drive, but nearly one-third (31%) of participants in the survey indicated some degree of diminished sexual interest. Recorded responses acknowledging a decrease in sex-drive were similar for respondents of both genders (28% females,

FIGURE 5a

Hours Per Week with Sex Offenders and Fatigue Experienced*
For those responding

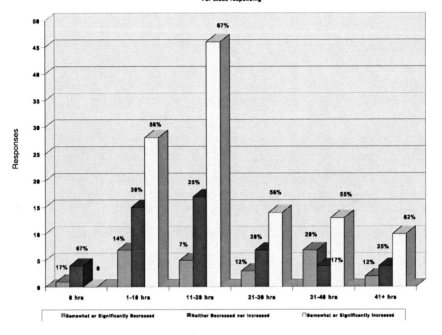

FIGURE 5b

Hours Per Week with Sex Offenders and Frustration Experienced
For those responding

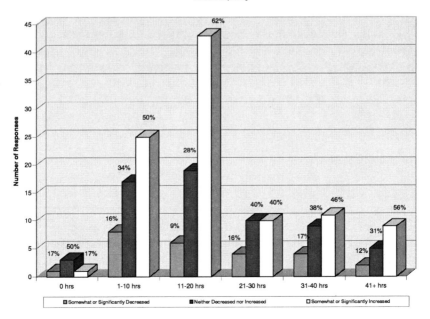

FIGURE 5c

Hours Per Week with Sex Offenders and Cynicism Experienced*
*For those responding

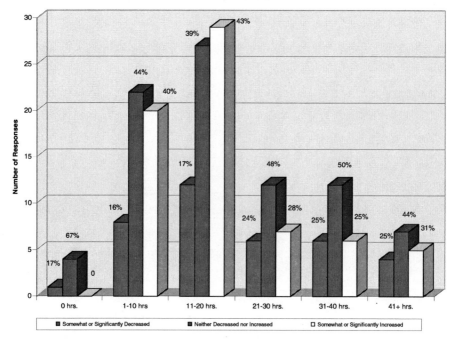

32% males). These findings lend support to responses compiled in a study conducted by Ellerby and colleagues (1993), despite variations in response syntax.

Similar responses were found for changes in body weight and physical exercise. Forty-one percent (41%) of respondents reported a decrease in physical activities, and 37% indicated an increase in body weight. Despite the impossibility of deriving causal relationships from this survey, recognizing that physical activity is often recommended for stress reduction is important. If generalizing the reported decrease in physical activity to the mental health profession were possible, many professionals could reduce burnout symptoms by using exercise as a readily accessible way to prevent or control stress.

Discussion

This study was an attempt to evaluate the personal impact of working with sex-abuse perpetrators. As evidenced by the information-collection process, no controls were provided to account for extraneous factors or events that may have contributed to the increase, decrease, or stability of burnout symptoms. In addition, the findings were not compared with a control sample to distinguish experiential differences between populations. The intent of the research was merely to collect subjective responses regarding personal and employment demographics, abuse characteristics, and reported changes in frequently identified burnout symptoms.

Although no causal relationship between providing therapy to sex-abuse perpetrators and burnout has been found, the responses to this survey suggest that individuals working with sex-abuse perpetrators are indeed subject to burnout. More than half of all respondents reported an increase in fatigue and frustration, and one-third of the respondents cited increases in cynicism, sleep disturbances, general irritability, and private time spent thinking about work. In addition, one-fourth of the survey respondents acknowledged an increased difficulty making decisions and an increase in depression and/or depressive episodes.

Job stress, or burnout, is apparently becoming more readily acknowledged in various workplaces. As for all employees, having access to stress-prevention and intervention services in the workplace is vital for sex-abuser treatment providers. Alaska's Department of Corrections might serve as an example for agencies willing to establish stress management programs in the workplace. The department developed a resource manual and made it available to probation officers working in sex-abuse programs (Alaska Department of Corrections, 1992). The manual contains qualitative descriptions of stress, burnout, critical-incident stress debriefing, and management methods according to the types of stress experienced.

Despite the limitations of this study, its findings confirm that sex-abuser treatment providers are apparently not immune to symptoms of burnout. Further, they suggest that clinicians with histories of abuse, particularly those with histories of sexual abuse, may be at a higher risk of experiencing burnout than other clinicians. Additional research is warranted and would prove useful to the professionals who treat sex-abuse perpetrators.

Conclusion

Although a causal relationship cannot be drawn from this study, results emphasize the need for focused research in this employment population. Providing treatment to sex-abuse perpetrators is a young profession but will be a long-term part of the human services field. Effective burnout prevention and intervention strategies will likely contribute to improved quality of service needed to combat the violence of sexual abuse. Employer-provided manuals and resources might be the first step toward actively managing job-related burnout for therapists who treat sex-abuse perpetrators.

Although causal relationships may be useful to research that focuses on burnout in the sex-abuser treatment provider, the initial concern must be prevention and intervention. Whatever the direct causes of burnout, many clinicians who work with sex-abuse perpetrators experience burnout symptoms. Without effective intervention, professional practice may be hindered and personal problems may develop among clinicians. The challenge of the profession is to develop a comprehensive understanding of the risk factors for burnout and the presentation, assessment, and management of singular or multiple symptoms. As Abel (1983) reminds us, if sex-abuser treatment providers are to be effective in preventing sexual violence, they must be aware of the high incidence of burnout among personnel and start prevention and management efforts.

References

Abel, G. (1983). Preventing men from becoming rapists. In G. S. Albee & H. Leightenberg (Eds.) *Promoting sexual responsibility and preventing sexual problems* (pp. 238-250). Hanover, NH: University Press of New England.

Ackerley, G., Burnell, J., Holder, D., & Kurdek, L. (1988). Burnout among licensed psychologists. *Professional Psychology: Research and Practice, 19*(6), 624-631.

Allen, B., & Brekke, K.E. (1995, October). *The process of transference/countertransference in the psychotherapeutic treatment of incarcerated sex offenders.* Paper presented at the meeting of the Association for the Treatment of Sexual Abusers, New Orleans, LA.

Bernard, M., Fuller, S., Robbins, E., & Shaw, M. (1989). *The Child Molester.* New York: Plenum.

Bloom, S.L. (1993). Vicarious traumatization and therapist self-care. *Traumatic Stress Points: News for the International Society for Traumatic Stress Studies, 7*(3), 3-4.

Briere, J. (1989). *Therapy for adults molested as children: Beyond survival.* New York: Springer.

Custer, G. (1994, October). Balance can counteract stress at work. *The APA Monitor, 27*(10), 49-50.

Edelwich, J., & Brodsky, A. (1980). *Burn-out: Stages of disillusionment in the helping professions.* New York: Human Sciences Press.

Ellerby, L., Gutkin, B., Smith, T., & Atkinson, R. (1993). *Treating sex offenders: The impact on clinicians.* Poster Presentation, 12th Annual Conference of the Association for the Treatment of Sexual Abusers, Boston, Massachusetts.

Farber, B. (1983). *Stress and burnout in the human service professions.* New York: Pergamon.

Farrenkopf, T. (1992). What happens to therapists who work with sex offenders? *Journal of Offender Rehabilitation, 18*(3/4), 217-223.

Freeman-Longo, P. (1993). [Burnout in Sex offender treatment providers]. Unpublished raw data.

Freudenberger, H.J. (1974). Staff burnout. *Journal of Social Issues, 30*(1), 159-165.

Grosch, W.N., & Olsen, D.C. (1994). *When helping starts to hurt: A new look at burnout among psychotherapists.* New York: Norton.

Hilton, Z.N., Jennings, K.T., Drugge, J., & Stephens, J. (1995) Childhood sexual abuse among clinicians working with sex offenders. *Journal of Interpersonal Violence, 10*(4), 525-532.

Kearns, B. (1995). Self-reflection in work with sex offenders: A process not just for therapists. *Journal of Child Sexual Abuse, 4*(1), 107-110.

Kestnbaum, J.D. (1984). Expectations for therapeutic growth: One factor is burnout. *Social Casework: The Journal of Contemporary Social Work, 65,* 374-377.

Maslach, C., & Jackson, S.E. (1982). Burnout in the health professional: A social psychological analysis. In G. Sanders & J. Suls (Eds.), *Social psychology of health and illness* (pp. 227-251). Hillsdale, NJ: Erlbaum.

Maslach, C., & Jackson, S.E. (1984). Burnout in organizational settings. In S. Oskamp (Ed.), *Applied social psychology annual 5: Applications in organizational settings* (pp.133-153). Beverly Hills, CA: Sage.

Maslach, C., & Jackson, S.E. (1986). *Maslach Burnout Inventory: Manual* (2nd ed.). Palo Alto, CA: Consulting Psychologists' Press.

McCann, I.L., & Pearlman, L.A. (1990). Vicarious traumatization: A framework for understanding the psychological effects of working with victims. *Journal of Traumatic Stress, 3*(1), 131-149.

McCann, I.L., & Pearlman, L.A. (1993). Vicarious traumatization: The emotional costs of working with survivors. *Treating Abuse Today, 3*(5), 28-31.

Peaslee, D.M. (1995). Countertransference with specific client populations: A comment on "The Treatment of Male Sexual Offenders." *Journal of Child Sexual Abuse, 4*(1), 111-115.

Pines, A., Aronson, E., & Kafry, D. (1981). *Burnout: From tedium to personal growth.* New York: Free Press.

Pines, A., & Maslach, C. (1978). Characteristics of staff burnout in mental health settings. *Hospital & Community Psychiatry, 29*(4), 233-237.

Pope, K.S., & Feldman-Summers, S. (1992). National survey of psychologists' sexual and physical abuse history and their evaluation of training and competence in these areas. *Professional Psychology: Research and Practice, 23,* 353-361.

Raquepaw, J., & Miller, R.S. (1989). Psychotherapist burnout: A componential analysis. *Professional Psychology: Research and Practice, 20,* 32-36.

Savicki, V., & Cooley, E. (January, 1987). The relationship of work environment and client contact to burnout in mental health professionals. *Journal of Counseling and Development, 65,* 249-253.

Scott, E. (December, 1989). Is there a criminal mind? *International Journal of Offender Therapy and Comparative Criminology, 33*(3) 215-226.

Skorupa, J., & Agresti, A.A. (1993) Ethical beliefs about burnout and continued professional practice. *Professional Psychology: Research and Practice, 24*(3), 281-285.

Sullivan, P.J. (1993). Occupational stress in psychiatric nursing. *Journal of Advanced Nursing, 18,* 591-601.

Taylor-Brown, S., Johnson, K.H., Hunter, K., & Rockowitz, R.J. (1981). Stress identification for social workers in health care: A preventative approach to burnout. *Social Work in Health Care, 7*(2), 91-100.

Yiu-kee, C., & Tang, C. S. (1995) Existential correlates of burnout among mental health professionals in Hong Kong. *Journal of Mental Health Counseling, 17*(2), 220-229.

Appendix A

This brief questionnaire was designed to assess how working with sex offenders may impact your life. Please answer all questions and return to the SAFER SOCIETY. You may direct suggestions or comments to: Stacey Bird, Safer Society, P.O. Box 340, Brandon, Vermont 05733; (802) 247-3132. Thank you for your participation.

PERSONAL IMPACT SURVEY

Unless otherwise directed, please select the one item that best classifies your response.

1. Please indicate your gender   ❏ female   ❏ male

2. Please indicate your age range   ❏ 20-25   ❏ 26-30   ❏ 31-35   ❏ 36-40   ❏ 41-45
      ❏ 46-50   ❏ 51-55   ❏ 56-60   ❏ 61 or more

3. Please indicate your *primary* job   ❏ therapist   ❏ probation/parole officer
      ❏ direct care staff   ❏ case manager/worker
      ❏ administrator/program manager
      ❏ other _____

4. Please indicate which *one* of the   ❏ private practice   ❏ residential/hospital
   following best describes your   ❏ day treatment   ❏ prison/correctional
   following best describes your   ❏ community mental health
      ❏ other _____

5. Please indicate the highest   ❏ Doctorate   ❏ Master's Degree
   degree that you have attained.   ❏ Bachelor's Degree   ❏ Associate's Degree
      ❏ High School Diploma
      ❏ Other_____

6. Are you responsible for the   ❏ yes   ❏ no
   supervision of staff?
   If yes, how many?   ❏ (number of staff) _____

7. How many years have you worked   ❏ 0-2   ❏ 3-5   ❏ 6-8   ❏ 9-11   ❏ 12-14
   in the mental health field?   ❏ 15 or more

8. How many years have you been   ❏ 0-2   ❏ 3-5   ❏ 6-8   ❏ 9-11   ❏ 12-4
   working with sex offenders?   ❏ 15 or more

9. How long (in hours) is your   ❏ 0-3   ❏ 4-6   ❏ 7-9   ❏ 10-12   ❏ 13 or more
   average work day?

10. How long (in hours) is your   ❏ 1-8   ❏ 9-16   ❏ 17-24   ❏ 25-32   ❏ 33-40
    average work week?   ❏ 41 or more

11. How many hours per week do   ❏ 0   ❏ 1-10   ❏ 11-20   ❏ 21-30   ❏ 31-40
    you spend working in direct   ❏ 41 or more
    contact with sex offender clients?

12. What percentage of your sex   ❏ 0   ❏ 1-15%   ❏ 16-30%   ❏ 31-45%   ❏ 46-60%
    offender clientele is male?   ❏ 61-75%   ❏ 76-90%   ❏ 91-100%

13. What is the age range of the   ❏ N/A   ❏ 1-9   ❏ 10-20   ❏ 21-30   ❏ 31-40
    majority of your male sex   ❏ 41 or more
    offender clientele?

Please turn to the next page

14. What percentage of your sex offender clientele is female? ❏ 0 ❏ 1-15% ❏ 16-30% ❏ 31-45% ❏ 46-60% ❏ 61-75% 76-90% ❏ 91-100%

15. What is the age range of the majority of your female sex offender clientele? ❏ N/A ❏ 1-9 ❏ 10-20 ❏ 21-30 ❏ 31-40 ❏ 41 or more

16. Is your wage/salary adequate for the work that you do? ❏ yes ❏ no

17. In a given calendar year, approximately how many hours of sex offender-specific training do you receive? ❏ 0-10 ❏ 11-20 ❏ 21-30 ❏ 31-40 ❏ 41-50 ❏ 51 or more

18. In the past year, have you experienced a highly stressful event in your personal life that is unrelated to your work? ❏ yes ❏ no

19. If you are an abuse survivor, please indicate the type(s) of abuse to which you have been subjected. ❏ sexual ❏ physical ❏ psychological ❏ other_____

20. Have you received treatment from a licensed therapist regarding your victimization issues? ❏ yes ❏ no

21. Based on your knowledge of sexually offensive behavior, have you ever questioned the appropriateness of any of your past sexual behavior? ❏ yes ❏ no

Please turn to the third and final page of this questionnaire.

Circle the number that best corresponds with your response.

Completely Disagree	Somewhat Disagree	Neither Disagree nor Agree	Somewhat Agree	Completely Agree
1	2	3	4	5

I am clear about what is expected of me in my workplace	1	2	3	4	5
I have been adequately trained to perform my job	1	2	3	4	5
My professional opinion is valued at my workplace	1	2	3	4	5
I am appropriately challenged at work	1	2	3	4	5
I find the community to be supportive of the work I do	1	2	3	4	5
I receive emotional support from other staff	1	2	3	4	5
I receive emotional support from my immediate supervisor	1	2	3	4	5
I find my family and/or close friends to be supportive of my work	1	2	3	4	5
My co-workers most often work as a team	1	2	3	4	5
I spend an adequate amount of time relaxing each day	1	2	3	4	5
I have a positive attitude toward work	1	2	3	4	5
I have diversity in my daily responsibilities at work	1	2	3	4	5
My job benefits the general well being of others	1	2	3	4	5
I am good at my job	1	2	3	4	5
My general well being is important to my supervisors/co-workers	1	2	3	4	5
I am subjected to physical harm at work	1	2	3	4	5
My physical work space is reasonably comfortable	1	2	3	4	5
I am allowed adequate time to perform my duties	1	2	3	4	5
I receive adequate supervision	1	2	3	4	5

Over the past year, to what extent have you experienced a change in the following? Please circle the one number that best represents your response.

Significantly Decreased	Somewhat Decreased	Neither Decreased Nor Increased	Somewhat Increased	Significantly Increased
1	2	3	4	5

Difficulty making decisions	1	2	3	4	5
Cynicism about life in general	1	2	3	4	5
Fatigue	1	2	3	4	5
Procrastination	1	2	3	4	5
Sleep disturbances	1	2	3	4	5
Absenteeism (from work)	1	2	3	4	5
General irritability	1	2	3	4	5
Self esteem	1	2	3	4	5
Ability to control anger	1	2	3	4	5
Social/leisure time with friends (non-work related)	1	2	3	4	5
Depression/depressive episodes	1	2	3	4	5
Feelings of frustration	1	2	3	4	5

Insensitivity to others	1	2	3	4	5
Private time spent thinking about work	1	2	3	4	5
Sex drive	1	2	3	4	5
Daily exercise	1	2	3	4	5
Body weight	1	2	3	4	5
Alcohol/drug use	1	2	3	4	5
Frequency of physical illness(es)	1	2	3	4	5
Confidence in personal safety	1	2	3	4	5
Feelings of helplessness	1	2	3	4	5
Positive thoughts/feelings regarding the future	1	2	3	4	5

2

Personal and Interpersonal Issues for Staff Working with Sexually Abusive Youth

STEVEN M. BENGIS, Ed.D., L.C.S.W.[1]

In the early 1970s, one of the first clinics to offer adolescent sex offender-specific treatment opened in Seattle, Washington. Since then, we have witnessed a rapid increase in the number of programs and practitioners dedicated to the treatment of juvenile sex offenders. The field has emphasized the development of treatment programs, refinement of diagnostic criteria and intervention techniques, and statewide interagency planning. Less emphasis has been placed on exploring the impact of this work on the individual practitioner.

This chapter explores this impact and seeks to raise awareness of the personal and interpersonal dimensions of this work to the same status that practitioners currently afford to client intervention, program development and outcome research. Once treatment providers have chosen to work in sex offender treatment, we enter what I can best describe as a "twilight world." This world alters our perceptions of daily events and, even more disturbingly, may change our inner lives—sometimes irrevocably. What we see when we walk down the street, what we think about in public places, what we fantasize, feel and/or fear often differs markedly from the experiences of others who do not experience the worlds in which we immerse ourselves.

Few practitioners work with sex abusers without becoming aware of the presence of new ideas, feelings, fantasies, impulses and urges directly related to this work. In spite of ourselves, we may discover inner imagery that simply will not go away or fantasies that parallel the acts described to us by our clients; we may also discover impulses, which, if acted upon, would put us in the same treatment programs that we now administer. For the sake of our own mental health and longevity in the field, we must discuss these di-

---

[1] Steven M. Bengis, Ed.D., is the director of the New England Adolescent Research Institute, Inc., in Holyoke, MA, a national trainer and consultant, and a former member of the National Task Force on Juvenile Sex Offending.

mensions of our work experience in the ways that we now talk about our clients' experiences.

Over the past seven years, discussions with colleagues and responses to my work on the personal and interpersonal effects suggest that very few of us spend much time discussing these psychic events honestly with supervisors, friends, or colleagues. Mostly, we live with these "occupational hazards" in isolation. We wonder about our own deviance; we worry about the implications for the psychic health of our fantasies and thoughts; we become too sensitized to being victimized; and at times, we become hyper-vigilant about both the safety of our children and our interactions with them.

The isolation and silence, rather than any objective knowledge about collegial norms, help foster feelings about our own "weirdness" or "deviance." The "twilight world" experiences identified above are far more common than most of us realize. Although the impact of this "twilight world" varies in fantasy content, specific bothersome images, types of impulses, and ranges of feelings, there are some general themes seem to resonate across the sex-offender-professional spectrum and across gender, ethnic, and sexual-preference lines. These common dimensions include: 1) mistrusting others' sexual behavior, especially people with regular access to children; 2) projecting possible abusive motivation onto innocuous interactions and events; 3) managing a range of feelings, including sadness for victims; fear, rage and disgust toward clients; and deep distress at the incidence of sexually abusive behavior occurring around us; 4) experiencing fleeting feelings of titillation or sexual arousal while listening to descriptions of abuse ranging from minor molestations to heinous sexual crimes; and 5) experiencing impulses to act out in sexually deviant ways.

Unfortunately, we do not have any statistically valid data related to the incidence of these experiences. If we had such data, I believe that the information might parallel the responses I received to the questionnaire that appears as Appendix A at the end of this chapter. Over the past seven years, I have distributed the questionnaire to several thousand trainees and, in percentages ranging from approximately 25% to 80%, respondents have answered positively to each of these questions. Although not methodologically sound from a research perspective, the percentages suggest a significant degree of common psychic impact related to working with sex offenders. Whether respondents perceived the impact as intrusive, disturbing, frightening or simply just present, practitioners should explore and integrate these effects as necessary components of work with sexually abusive individuals.

Integrating this hidden, or "shadow," side of our psyches is important to our own psychological health and may enhance our work with abused and abusing clients. Leading clients through the complex realities of deviant arousal, sexual fantasy, thinking errors, and dangerous and illegal impulses is difficult when we cannot draw on our own experiences with those dimensions of inner reality. Sex-offender treatment, particularly for adolescents, is more than the communication of information about assault cycles, mutually desired and forced sex, or relapse prevention. Treatment involves sharing an appreciation for the power of deviant arousal, the role of fantasy in everyday life, the pull of addictive feelings, and the confusion that the addictive "False Self"[2] can play in identity formation. Further, it involves an appreciation for the complex process of integrating the "shadow" components into psychic reality without concretizing them in abusive behaviors.

Most of us struggle with issues of power, control, impulsiveness, addictive impulses or behaviors, and thinking errors. As far as we can draw on these struggles and experiences to help construct our interactions with these youth, we can more effectively help them in their transition from sexually abusive to sexually appropriate behavior. I do not suggest that we share naively either our experiences or our inner realities with our clients other than at carefully chosen and appropriate therapeutic moments; however, we should use our knowledge of these processes and our experiences with integrating them as important resources to help guide our interventions with clients.

Although an honest inner inventory should precede any use of our experiences in treatment, any request for such honesty may provoke anxiety. We may not like all that we find inside ourselves. The presence of certain fantasies, impulses, or urges may embarrass us. We may find it impossible to reconcile parts of this inner world with our rational belief systems or our political orientations. Yet, despite the inconsistencies, the embarrassments and even the fears that honest self-exploration often elicits, usually I think such exploration is helpful. An unbiased examination of our inner lives may help us to become less inflated, less repressed, or less fearful. It may also make us a bit more tolerant and accepting of our own human frailty and that of abusive youth.

My aim is to encourage self-reflection. I write about a topic that, though apparently relevant for many practitioners, is extremely personal and lacks quantitative research that would establish practitioner norms. Therefore, I am aware that the examples and personal anecdotes I have chosen may differ markedly from the experiences of some readers. This circumstance is particularly true if the reader is not, like the author, white, heterosexual and male. For example, I know that many of my fantasies, impulses and emotional responses to clients' stories differ markedly from those of my female colleagues. In addition, although I have not discussed it with them, I do not assume that my experiences parallel those of gay or minority practitioners. Given the variety of individual practitioner inner reality, I offer the anecdotes or personal experiences I write about only as examples of a type or genre of experience rather than as an indication of the universality of the particular experiences. Further, in validating and expressing tolerance

---

[2] The addictive "False Self" is the illusion of the addict that he/she is really more him/herself when engaging in addictive behaviors than he/she is at any other time. It is the pull of excitement, arousal and power, that creates the illusion that only when the addict engages in these addictive behaviors can his/her true (actually "false") self emerge. At other times, he/she is depressed, bored, and self-derogatory, feelings which the addicted person cannot believe really are part of his/her "true" identity.

for a range of inner experiences, I want to be clear about the need to differentiate inner reality from outer behavior. We should construe nothing that I write here as a license to act out the fantasies or impulses that this work may generate.

With that as a caveat, note that the scenes in the guided fantasy in Appendix B have been drawn from actual experiences of workshop participants, trainees, or colleagues, although the sequenced scenario is fictional. The fantasy does, however, reflect a typical, although intense, day in the life of a sex offender practitioner who works as an abuse investigator and a group treatment leader. Please reflect for a moment on the vivid imagery, or the thoughts, feelings, fears, or fantasies elicited. The presence of those psychic dimensions, not their specific characteristics, is most relevant to this analysis.

Images

Some years ago, Tom, a fifteen-year-old offender, sat impassively describing the details of his rape of his prepubescent sister to a female colleague of mine. At her request, he described in detail how he had dragged his child victim by the ankles down a staircase and then raped her when they reached the bottom. As he described the events, my colleague formed these words into images. She then listened with the inner image of a small child's head bouncing from one step to the next one as the child was being dragged down the stairs. The images did not last very long, and she could make an appropriate professional response and continue with the interview.

That night, as she drove home, the images recurred. They returned as she prepared to go to sleep and again at various moments over the next three months. Bang, bang, bang: the child's head slammed against each stair as she was pulled down. My colleague could not get rid of that mental image. Although not debilitating, the recurrence of the imagery was disturbing and stressful.

Whatever the specific details of the image or the meaning of those images to our own psychology, most of us have heard a story from an offender that has left us with imagery that has imposed itself upon our consciousness in disturbing ways. At times, those images are momentary; at other times, as with the example above, they remain for a long time.

One of the most powerful examples of the effect of sex offender imagery in my own life relates to the guided fantasy in Appendix B. The gesture of the small child picked up by the police officer (e.g., wrenching away and simultaneously pushing her head into the officer's lap) is one I watched on a film of an interview of a male incest offender's family, including his infant victim. In that film, the child gestured in a manner identical to that described in the guided fantasy, and viewers were informed that the offender had intermittently substituted his penis for a bottle while feeding the child. Within that single gesture, a pre-verbal child portrayed all the complexity and horror of that kind of confusing, abusive act. I could not rid my psyche of that image for nine years. For weeks after I viewed that film, the image repeated itself often in my head. Almost every time it recurs, I experience a shudder in my body. Through the imagery, the trauma that child experienced has become a visceral experience for me.

Why has this image remained with me over the years, as opposed to other images that might have had a similar impact? I do not know, nor is the answer important to the point I wish to make. What matters is that eventually most of us in the field find ourselves dealing with distressing, repetitive imagery that contains feeling and meaning for us. Although not all the images are frightening and negative, their mere presence can be disturbing, because they often arise unbidden from outside our consciousness. Finding healthy, creative and integrating ways to deal with such images is one challenge sex-offender practitioners face.

Feelings

What do we do with the feelings that arise as we listen to an offender describe his sexual molestation of a child without a trace of remorse or the slightest recognition of the impact of that event on the child's life? How do we manage our sense of outrage, or our anger, sadness, and disgust when an offender refuses either to accept responsibility for his acts, or to perceive the "insanity" of seeing his behavior as a "reasonable response" to the "sexually provocative" actions of the three-year-old sitting in his lap?

In 1988, I participated in a two-day training session in Maine. During one session, a therapist treating victims showed a movie in which an adult pedophile graphically described not only his own sexually abusive crimes, but also his long history of victimization by both his father and an aunt. As I watched the movie, I began to feel nauseous and constricted. I felt as though I were suffocating and that my world was "flip-flopping" in Alice-in-Wonderland style. Everything sacred was being profaned. Everything beautiful and enriching about childhood and sexuality was becoming ugly and twisted. The unacceptable was commonplace, and the intolerable was almost normal. I felt slightly crazy. All I wanted to do was get outside and be with the sunlight and the flowers. I had an urgent impulse to get to a phone and reconnect with my wife. That moment passed, and after a break during which I rather shakily walked alone outside, I returned to the auditorium and made my presentation.

Although the intensity of that particular experience exceeded the norm for my own work, it typified the emotional context within which our work takes place. One cannot listen to the sexually abusive events described by victims and offenders without eventually being inundated with intense feelings. Clinicians can simply note some of those feelings, catalogue them, and allow them to dissipate. Others must either be expressed to clients, colleagues, spouses or friends, or examined with thoroughness and depth. At the least, such feelings must be honored and accepted as having a place within our psychic lives. If we try to ignore or repress them, we run the risk of "burn out," numbness, or other psychic damage.

A few cautionary words about my advocacy for emotional expressiveness with clients: I believe that offenders need to hear our anger, outrage, and anguish over the pain they have caused victims. They need to be confronted forcefully with a morality and ethical framework differing drastically from the internalized abusive norms substituting for conscience in so many of them. They need to see our sadness at their own victimization and at appropriate moments, they may also need to see our vulnerability, particularly if we attempt to provide male role models. I believe that our own humanity must become part of our treatment interventions. I also believe that finding appropriate ways and times to express our feelings to clients may be a prerequisite to our own long-term survival in this work. However, although I believe that expressing certain feelings to clients appropriately is essential, we do not have license to act out or to be abusive or shaming. Expressing strong feelings professionally, honestly and with integrity is not always easy. If a clinician tends to "lose it" when filled with emotions, then perhaps a better idea is to take time to transform raw emotion into differentiated feeling, or work out such issues with a supervisor before expressing emotion-laden responses to clients.

Most important, however, we must find ways to acknowledge our feelings to ourselves, to share our feelings with our colleagues and supervisors when the emotions become too intense or overwhelming to manage alone, and to express those feelings to clients in appropriate and meaningful ways when the opportunity to do so presents itself. Acknowledgment, sharing and expression may be the basic components of emotional first aid for all of us.

Feelings of Sexual Arousal

Certain feelings may be so disturbing that we can barely acknowledge them to ourselves, let alone share them with other colleagues or supervisors. Expressing them to clients would be inappropriate. For example, we hear a story and almost in spite or ourselves feel a tinge of sexual arousal and excitement. We may hastily quash the sensation, or dismiss or deny its presence. Nevertheless, we know that it happened. How can we make sense of the experience? How can we integrate it with our self-image, political values, and professional identities?

Sex-offender treatment providers may become upset the first time they honestly acknowledge to themselves that a description of a rape or the thought of a sexual act with a child has aroused them. Often, self-recrimination and questioning follow the experience. "What is the matter with me?" "Am I disturbed or sick?" "Are all my stated beliefs, values, and politics merely a faHade behind which stands the true perverted self?" Perhaps the scariest question of all may be, "Am I capable of committing the same acts?" Once asked, such questions are not always easily answered. We may push them out of our heads, label them as ridiculous, or rationalize their presence; however, if my own experience is any indication, the questions lurk in the back of our minds like stalking beasts. Once these questions are formulated, our psychological health is best served by honestly coming to grips with the answers.

For some practitioners, the answers may be simple; for others, they may be complex or sufficiently revealing to require that we do additional intense work on ourselves in therapy. Finally, the answers may suggest that we have entered this field for highly unethical and questionable reasons; if we have any integrity, that revelation should motivate us to find other employment. For most of us, however, I believe the answers will relieve us and will lead to a deeper integration of the "dark side" of our own natures. For those of us who have chosen to engage in this work, I believe we need to have the courage to ask and then answer honestly even the disquieting and embarrassing questions.

To put sexual arousal into a context less tied to our identities, self-concept, or self-esteem may be useful. At any given moment as we listen to sexually explicit material, we may not be in touch with the victim's realities. We may translate what we hear into our own fantasies, as clients and many other people do. For example, I recently made a presentation to school teachers about sexual abuse. During the conversation, a sex education teacher spoke about the increasing number of stories she was hearing from young boys about sexually aggressive and abusive females. At that point, a male teacher jokingly asked, "Where were those females when I was growing up?" Although made in jest, the comment was both revealing and poignant because it gave us an opportunity to explore the differences between the fantasies generated by stories of sexual abuse and the reality of the abuse itself. Our inability to differentiate different levels of reality, I believe, has generated the discomfort so many of us feel about the sexual arousal that providing sex-abuse treatment may generate.

My guess was that the male teacher who made the comment had experienced a moment of excitement and sexual arousal at the thought of a young woman assertively "taking" sex from him. So many of us remember vividly the discomfort, embarrassment and difficulty of our first sexual experiences as adolescents. What were we supposed to do? What were we supposed to say? Would we be "male" enough? Would we do it right? The thought of meeting a woman or age-peer who would guide us through our first experience, or who would simply "do it" to us so we would not have to take any responsibility at all was enticing.

Those fantasies never included fear, or embarrassment, or impotence, or lack of control. They were fantasies in which we would have all our questions answered without ever having to ask them. We could have all the sexual experiences we wondered about without having to take responsibility for wanting them. We would learn about all the techniques we had heard about without having to "bumble" along foolishly to figure them out. Those fantasies did not concern sexual abuse. They were "quasi- consenting" fantasies, i.e., "Take me, I'm all yours." However, rape or "quasi-rape" fantasies have nothing to do with actual rape. Within our "rape" fantasies we generally feel safe, aroused, and excited. Within those fantasies, we *choose* to be "taken." We limit the fear or pain we experience to levels commensurate with our own arousal patterns and sexual interests. In our fantasies, partners or other people do not smother us, and we do not feel terrified or invaded.

In the moment that the sex-education teacher began talking about sexually abusive female teenagers, I do not believe that the male teacher responded to the realities of that story, but to the realities of his own fantasy life. Frequently, I believe that a similar inner lack of differentiation causes arousal during descriptions of sexually abusive acts; however, unlike offenders who cannot, or choose not to, make such differentiations and do act on fantasies with relative disregard for the effects on a victim, most of us would not be capable of acting on our non-consenting, sexually arousing fantasies. Once we understand the reality of victim impact and the consequences to the victims' lives and to our own, the arousal that we may have initially experienced generally dissipates, and an appropriate emotional reaction replaces it.

I do not believe we should worry much about moments of sexual arousal by even the most "deviant" sexual material. We should only become concerned if, over time, we become preoccupied with deviant fantasies or more aroused by images of non-consenting sexual acts than by consenting-sex images. Once this becomes the case, it is probably time to seek counseling. In other circumstances, I think we should be aware of the fantasies and be gentle with ourselves about their presence. Though reflecting on the nature of our sexual fantasies may be useful, we should also remember that fantasies are not offenses, and the role of fantasy in psychic life relates more to psychic balance than it does to conventions of correct behavior.

In presenting this paradigm for addressing practitioners' intermittent sexual arousal during the work, I have avoided exploring the important sociological, political and economic relationships of arousal, objectification, impersonal sex and male oppression of women and children. Exploration and alteration of these patterns and relationships may ultimately lead to an alteration in male arousal responses. However, without such a change, political beliefs or values may too easily become superego functions through which we engage in debilitating forms of repression, self-blame and shaming. Male arousal is complex and integrally woven into the fabric of our culture. Cultural conditioning does not change simply because we "will it to." The professional working with sexual deviancy should honor and recognize the truth of his or her experience rather than repress, avoid or deny it because that experience does not conform to an objective value or belief that he or she holds. Repression and denial never lead to transformation.

We may not have much respect for some of our responses, we may wish we were different, or we may be working on our sexuality. Nevertheless, we must start from where we are, and in this instance, that means observing, noting, and acknowledging the existence of sexual arousal in our professional lives.

Impulses and Urges

In addition to the images, thoughts and feelings that we must manage, we must also, at times, manage very disturbing impulses and urges. When they occur, such impulses seem to put us at the edge of the boundary between deviant thoughts or feelings and sexually abusive, criminal or highly inappropriate behavior. I have found the impulses generated by this work to be the scariest, most difficult inner experiences with which to deal, more so than images, fantasies or feelings.

Impulses, sexual or other, often occur spontaneously. I drive over a steep mountain road with few guardrails and have a sudden impulse to turn the steering wheel sharply to the left or right, hurtling myself to an almost certain death. Similarly, as I drive down the road and see a motorcycle or giant truck driving in the opposite direction, I have an urge to swerve into its path, either smashing the motorcycle or being smashed by the truck; closer to my topic, I may ride in an elevator alone with an attractive female stranger and have an impulse to grab her, tear her clothes off and passionately fondle her before the door opens.

About a year ago, I worked with a juvenile sex offender whose *modus operandi* included sneaking up behind women on the street, grabbing their posteriors, and then running away and hiding. One day, after listening to those stories over several weeks as part of his group introductions, I was walking behind an attractive woman and had a very strong impulse to reach out and grab her as the client had described doing. The impulse was fleeting and was followed almost instantaneously by the strong inner voice of reality warning me about both consequences and victim impact; however, there was also a moment of excitement and arousal.

In the instant between impulse and action, the inhibiting mechanisms that prevent acting out seem very fragile, and the choice of action seems almost instinctive rather than rational or planned. I suspect that in those very private moments, when no one knows our inner experience, when our impulse is such that acting on it would change the entire scope of our lives or take life itself, all that we are and all that we believe come into play so quickly, both cognitively and emotionally, that we are unaware of all the beliefs, values and ego constructs that stand between the impulse and the action. When we experience the impulse, however, it seems so real that it generates fear and an almost detached perverse interest. We may even experience an adrenaline "rush" with its concomitant physical effects, such as faster heartbeat or tingling, sweaty hands.

Once the moment has passed and we safely pass the guardrail or the motorcycle or step off the elevator, we are left to ponder or integrate that impulsive moment. We ask ourselves: "How close was I *really* to swerving off the bridge, annihilating the motorcyclist, or sexually molesting the stranger? What is the matter with me that I even have these impulses? Am I secretly suicidal, homicidal, or sexually abusive?" I believe and sincerely hope that for most of us, the answer to these questions is "No." The reasons for the impulses are complex and beyond the purpose and scope of this analysis. Personally, their presence has made me more appreciative of both the power of the inner world that we ask offenders to manage and the importance of developing inner constructs that interpose themselves between impulse and action.

Even when our response to an impulse is appropriate, however, the experience of the impulse may be embarrassing and/or distressing even if we are the only ones who know about it. The specific impulses that practitioners experience may vary, depending upon gender, sexual preference, socialization, and experience. I think that many practitioners will at some point experience sexually inappropriate impulses and concomitant disconcerting doubts about identity. Dealing with such impulses is one of the more disturbing occupational hazards associated with this work, but one that places us at the center of the world that offender clients must always confront. The more we have experienced that world ourselves, the more likely it is that we can probably help offenders adequately cope with it.

Fantasies

Besides thoughts, feelings, images, and impulses, providing sex-offender treatment may also generate vivid fantasies. Those fantasies may be frightening, aggressive, arousing, deviant, sad or scary. They may be brief or extended; they may arise when the clinician walks down the street after dark and a man walks behind her; when a practitioner drops his child off at a day-care center and sees a male counselor put his hand innocuously over the child's shoulder; when a therapist is listening to offenders speak, or when sitting quietly by oneself after a hard day's work; when a treatment provider is in bed with a lover or rolling on the ground with his or her child. Dealing with such fantasies also becomes part of the prerequisites for successfully negotiating the "twilight world" of sex-abuse work.

For example, recently I walked into the home of my child's day-care provider and saw him holding my son on his lap reading. I had a brief fantasy of him sexually abusing my son. Perhaps other parents outside the sexual abuse treatment field might have had a similar fantasy, since so many parents live with the fears imposed by having to leave their children with people they can never know well enough. The fantasy is both informed by my work as a sex-abuser practitioner (which validates the potential truth of my imaginings), and complicated by that work experience. Not only does the fantasy enter my consciousness, but its presence fosters a range of other thoughts, e.g., questioning whether I should say something about what is probably a very innocuous moment or wondering, "What's the matter with me? Do I have to turn everything into something perverted? What if I am minimizing, and this really is inappropriate? Should I ask some explorative questions?" Generally, the moment passes, I say nothing, the fantasy is replaced with something else, and life moves on. The interplay of an informed consciousness and our fantasy lives can be most disconcerting.

Another example: I was on a plane on my way to a training session. A very attractive flight attendant excused herself as she leaned over me to pass a drink to another passenger. I had a brief non-consenting sexual fantasy, felt both excited and frightened by it, and the moment passed. I would not be surprised if half the male passengers on the plane had similar types of fantasies during that flight. However, a litany of self-reflective comments stemming from my work followed my fantasy. "You know what acting on that fantasy would mean. You are engaging in thinking errors. If you were really committed to this work, you would not allow yourself to have these fantasies. This work is making a cesspool of your mind. Refocus! This is not healthy!"

Most people "manage" an active fantasy life. At times, they share certain fantasies with lovers, spouses or friends; at other times, they lock up their fantasies and enjoy them privately in their "closet" and pay little attention to countless others. Although sex-abuse treatment practitioners are no different, immersion in the field creates a hyper-vigilance or hypersensitivity to fantasies that parallel or imitate topics with which our daily professional lives are involved. Although many people experience sexual fantasies that border on the abusive, I believe it is more disconcerting to have such fantasies when one's days are spent treating abusers, speaking out against sexual abuse, correcting fantasy journals, and demanding honesty and accountability from clients. Most people experience violent fantasies, but when those violent fantasies are directed at our own clients and involve very brutal and sadistic acts, our commitment to treatment, healing, and humanistic values may come into question.

It is not the presence of the fantasy, but the relationship between the fantasy, the work, and consciousness that creates stress. Also, we may: 1) experience such fantasies more often than the average person; 2) become preoccupied with fantasies of victimizing or being victimized; 3) struggle to stop our fantasy lives from mimicking topics we confront as professionals; or 4) follow each fantasy with conscious reflections that may generate inner conflict. Sometimes the reflections are brief; sometimes the litany goes on for a while; and sometimes we ignore or repress the reflective thoughts. Rarely, however, are we free from consciousness and the running of the "inner tape."

Consciousness can often feel like a burden, and in instances like the ones described above, it often becomes one. As practitioners whose daily lives are immersed in deviant material, learning to allow, monitor, reflect on, disregard, enjoy, and/or integrate fantasies "goes with the territory" of this work. Whether our fantasies are sexual or violent, aggressive or aggrieved, fleeting or extended, exploring and integrating them are challenges faced by most practitioners in this field.

Alterations in Our World View
And Our Relationships with Loved Ones

The "twilight" sex-abuser world may irrevocably alter our relationships to strangers, to friends, lovers and spouses, and to our children. Our "twilight world" experiences leave us mistrustful. Whom do we know well enough to be sure they will not molest — the pediatrician, the teacher, the religious professional? What child care agency screens its staff carefully enough to exclude a determined pedophile? What teenage neighbor babysitter is beyond suspicion? What giggle between playmates in an upstairs bedroom can be guaranteed to suggest only appropriate play?

Recently, I read a front-page article in our local newspaper extolling the virtues of a seventy-five-year-old man who had devoted his life to work with the

Boy Scouts. The picture showed him surrounded by adoring young children. "Probably a perp who used his position to gain access to victims," I thought with some self-reproach.

Some months ago, I sat on a bus watching a grandfather playfully bounce his three- or four-year-old granddaughter on his knee as she giggled in delight. I noticed the warm smiles of several passengers around me. While I smiled, part of me wondered if he were becoming aroused from the experience, and wondered further what other "games" he might be playing with the child. An inner monologue immediately followed the thought: "Knock it off," I said to myself. "Yeah, but who knows? You may be right."

When I walked through a grocery store recently and saw a father with his arm draped over the shoulder of his young daughter, I wondered what fantasies were going through his mind. When my then-ten-year-old stepdaughter visited our school, and I heard giggles from her play in the basement playroom with our twenty-two-year-old janitor, I nervously paced in my office, wondering if I should go down to check on the type of games they were playing.

When that same stepdaughter asked me if she could stay overnight at a local roller skating rink for an adult-chaperoned sleep-over skate with many of her friends, it took great restraint not to shout "Are you crazy? Do you have any idea how many perps hang out in places like that?" Instead, with what I believed was calm objectivity, but which later my stepdaughter told me was transparent anxiety, I asked lots of questions. "Did anybody just hang around and not skate? How old is the oldest kid allowed into this party? How would she deal with someone whom she did not know asking her to join him to play video games?" The examples are myriad. The concerns cross my mind almost daily. The thoughts and anxieties arise every time my six-year-old child visits someone new, or we decide that we have to hire a new baby sitter.

Although these observations and the excessive or perhaps appropriate vigilance around caretakers and babysitters may not seem distressing, the change in patterns of relating to lovers, spouses, and children may be. I know practitioners who have found themselves unable to have sex for periods of time during which they were working to sort through their newly imposing inner lives. I know practitioners who no longer give their small children baths because they once had a moment of sexual arousal while bathing them. I know colleagues who can no longer wrestle with their children without editing the inner voice that says, "Well, you know this is how abusers gain access to victims. Be careful of your hands. Where is that leg going?" I know practitioners who cannot share the realities of work experiences with partners who think they are crazy to work with the sex offender population. These are the realities of engaging in this work, and some of us need help navigating through them. What are we doing to help each other? How can we help reframe some of the inner dialogue that makes these experiences far more debilitating than they need to be?

Although many colleagues have inner experiences that cause distress, I know others who have learned to share some of their fantasies with their partners and have enjoyed some delightful sexual moments for having taken that risk. I know other colleagues who have found ways to talk with their children about their work and its concomitant fears and deepened those relationships by doing so. Years after the event I described in our school with my stepdaughter, I talked to her about what it was like to grow up with me and her mother who is also in the sexual abuse treatment field. To my great relief, she told me it had always made her feel safer and somewhat proud that we knew so much. She also told me that often she just ignored us when we got too carried away with our anxieties (so much for my own hubris about affecting my children!). The changes in our relationships are not always negative, if we can acknowledge and integrate them.

Conclusion

In almost every training session I have conducted on this topic, I have seen visible relief in the faces of some attenders as we explore these topics. Invariably, someone approaches me after the training to tell me that it was the first time anyone had talked to them about what had become a disconcerting or deeply distressing aspect of the work. Few of us have so thoroughly integrated our own sexuality and our own psyches that some level of open discussion of these matters would not prove beneficial.

Most practitioners with any longevity in the field have learned to cope with 1) increased vigilance; 2) higher-than-average levels of anxiety about our children; 3) projections of abusive motivation onto innocuous events; 4) and hypersensitivity to even the slightest hint of sexual arousal or inappropriate touching. For other practitioners, however, particularly those just beginning to treat sexually abusive clients, we should provide a context for working through the potential "inner land mines." We need not be intrusive, and we should never demand self-disclosure. By naming some issues in the abstract and by sharing, in a general way, our own experiences with these dimensions of reality, however, we can at least "normalize" their existence and leave open the door for future exploration. Just as the many new books about sex-abuse treatment have made entry into the field for new practitioners much easier than it was twenty years ago, the willingness of seasoned sex-abuse treatment practitioners to speak about such experiences will make it easier for new colleagues to navigate through the difficult dimensions of this work safely.

I think it is important that each practitioner, as part of this internal navigation, honestly address his or her reasons for working with this specific client population. Given the trauma generated by sexual violence and the potential for prevention that early intervention provides, at one level, the answer to the question of motivation seems obvious. The violence of perpetrators outrages us and makes us committed to preventing further abuse through appropriate legal and treatment interventions. In addition, the creativity in and newness of the field offers professional challenges and rewards, both of which can be compelling;

however, ultimately neither of these answers suffices. A practitioner could mitigate a range of equally appalling social ills through similarly committed intervention such as counseling AIDS victims, male batterers, or the physically challenged, and such work would provide similar professional opportunities.

Ultimately, I think the answer to the question "Why choose to work with sex abusers?" is, for most of us, more personal and connected to our own psyches, unresolved issues, and inner journeys than other treatment areas. These more personal reasons do not negate our altruism, diminish the value or importance of our commitment, or suggest perverse natures. Answering this question, however, does impose a need to adopt the same principles of honesty, avoidance of minimization or denial, and acceptance of responsibility that we demand daily of abusive clients.

By focusing on some stressors unique to work with this population, I do not mean to negate the need to address other aspects of stress also experienced by other professionals not involved in sex-abuse treatment work. Additionally, I do not mean to disregard the importance of more traditional types of self-care, such as taking time off from work, exercising, maintaining a healthy diet, developing non-work-related interests, spending sufficient time with friends and family, or meditating. As important as they are, however, those types of self-nurturance are addressed in many other forums by other professionals. The unique aspects of the images, feelings, fantasies, impulses, and urges represent the hidden sources of stress in our work that we must explore if maintaining longevity in the field is a professional goal. I sincerely hope that this brief analysis will contribute to that exploration and that other professionals — women, minorities, non-heterosexuals — will begin to share and write about their experiences. By such exploration, I believe we will achieve a higher and healthier level of consciousness about our work than many experience now. I believe that this will also result in better work with clients and a higher level of safety for our communities than currently exists.

Appendix A

Questionnaire

Instructions: Please answer the following items with a yes or no.

1.____ Since I started working in the sex abuse/abuser field there have been certain images (i.e., pictures in my mind) that were never there before I began this work.

2.____ There have been times when I have been bothered by the presence of these images, but I consider them part of the job and ignore them most of the time.

3.____ There have been many strong feelings that I have had to deal with as a result of working in the abuse/abuser field.

4.____ I am generally able to talk about these feelings.

5.____ There are new fantasies that I have had as a result of being in this field.

6.____ Some of these fantasies involve sexually deviant acts.

7.____ Some of these fantasies I have had for the first time as a result of doing this work.

8.____ There have been times when I was troubled by the presence of these fantasies and wondered if there was something wrong with me.

9.____ Being in this field has changed the way I think about and relate to children (i.e. my own child(ren), other children with whom I have a close relationship). This change could be in the way I touch, an increase in fear or paranoia about safety issues, concerns about my own potential for deviant behavior with children, concerns about new sexual fantasies I have about children, etc.

10.___ In the past six months, I have discussed the issues which the above questions address with a supervisor.

Appendix B
Guided Fantasy

In preparation for this guided fantasy experience I would like to ask you to find a quiet space where you will not be disturbed and to devote about fifteen minutes of uninterrupted time to this next task. Once you are ready, read the following descriptions, a section at a time, until the text says STOP. Once you have stopped reading, please note your reactions, feelings, and thoughts for that particular passage. As you do so, please adopt a nonjudgmental and noneditorial perspective. We are not responsible for the existence of thoughts, feelings, fantasies, or impulses. These dimensions of inner reality are determined more by social custom and socialization, education, and unconscious forces than by any conscious intent. Our inner world is a bit like a movie. We may not like or respect or even want to acknowledge that such movies are playing inside of us. We may choose to close our eyes during certain scenes, or attempt to walk out of the theater all together, but regardless of our responses, those movies are playing within us. The more we attempt to ignore or repress them, the more powerful those movies become. Ignoring or repressing inner reality is not a particularly useful approach. It is better to be in relationship to our inner lives in as conscious, responsible, and ethical a manner as possible. So please proceed. Do not censure, do not judge; just observe and note your reactions.

When you have completed the guided fantasy, please return to the text.

1. You receive a report from a school of a thirteen-year-old girl who is experiencing vaginal bleeding. The school nurse suspects abuse. You are asked to do an investigation. You call the police and set a time to meet a police investigator to join with you. You also call the family to set a time to meet with the alleged victim, the mother and the father. The family seems very reticent to see you, but finally agrees. You do not have time to coordinate your plans with the police officer and meet him/her for the first time, ten minutes before you are scheduled to leave together to conduct the investigation.

STOP

2. The family lives on a very remote country road. You have virtually no background information on the family. As you drive up a long dirt driveway you see old junk cars strewn around the yard along with some empty beer cans and children's toys. The house is in bad repair and there are two dogs barking loudly as you knock at the door.

STOP

3. A woman in her late twenties opens the door very tentatively. She lets you in and a stale odor of liquor and urine emanates from the house. The place is a

mess, you notice a small child lying quietly on the couch and the thirteen-year-old sitting sullenly in the kitchen. Mom is disheveled with a hint of a bruise around her eye. As you look around the living room you notice a shotgun in the corner and some hunting rifles on a rack. Dad is not at home.

STOP

4. The police officer speaks with the mother and you speak with the thirteen-year-old. The mother breaks down crying. She states that her oldest son, aged sixteen, abused her daughter and that her husband has physically hit her on numerous occasions, particularly when he is drunk. She asks for protection and help. She also says that her husband will kill her if he finds out she said anything.

STOP

5. The police officer goes to sit with the two-year-old on the couch. He picks the child up in the air to play. The child twists sharply in his arms, as if to wrench away, and simultaneously pushes his head into the officer's lap. The officer picks the child up and the behavior is repeated.

STOP

6. You both tell the mother that you will try to get her into an emergency shelter and to help her protect her family, but first you need to check in at the office to see what beds are available. You urge her to get in the car with you and assure her that you will do everything possible to keep her and the family safe. She agrees, and you drive out quickly with the woman and her two children in the car.

STOP

7. You enter the office and talk with your supervisor about the case. As you describe the behavior of the infant, the supervisor doesn't see anything strange about it and seems skeptical about your concern about sexual abuse. There are no beds available in the shelter for battered women. You want to have the youthful offender and the father removed from the home, but the process is too lengthy and complicated. You find that there are no emergency beds for children for the next three days.

STOP

8. You contact the woman again and tell her you will keep looking for a safe place for her and her family and that you will get back to her by early

evening. In the afternoon you co-lead a sex-offender group. During the group a male abuser describes his m.o. for gaining access to his child victims. He describes how he plays games with them, gets them into wrestling activities and then begins to touch their genitals, seemingly "by accident." He also describes how small children often seduce him by running around the house naked, sitting in his lap, wriggling around and arousing him. He states that it is not his fault.

STOP

9. You tie up your work for the day, still unable to find an emergency bed. You contact the mother of the abused thirteen-year-old, give her as much verbal support as possible, and promise to be back in touch in the morning. You drive home. You are married and have two small children of your own. Your spouse works in a computer consulting business and has never understood why you work with offenders. She/he thinks it's all a bit perverted, but loves you and knows how important the work is to you. Whenever you have tried to share the work with your spouse, it has ended in a fight, so you have both agreed not to talk about it. As you open the door, your spouse is excited and happy about a wonderful day he/she has had and lightly asks you how you are.

STOP

10. You give your spouse a hug, make a passing remark about a difficult day, and see your two children racing around the living room. It is a hot summer day, they have just been playing in the backyard sprinkler and are running around naked. You go to hug them, and they jump all over you delighted to see you. The kids are three and five. One of them jumps on your back asking for a pony ride while the other playfully pushes you to the ground.

STOP

11. You grab them both and throw them around. As you all roll on the floor, one of the kids plops herself on top of you wriggling around playfully. As she does this, her leg falls in your crotch and accidentally rubs against your genitals. You experience a moment of sexual arousal.

STOP (Try to imagine how you would feel and what you would do.)

12. You gradually extricate yourself from the game and tell the kids to get ready for their bath. As you have always done, you help wash them, including being certain their genital area is washed.

STOP

13. When the kids are in bed and after you have cleared up some left over details and read the paper, you get ready for bed. Your spouse makes it clear he/she wants to make love. You are filled with thoughts, images, feelings. You want to talk first but know from experience what will happen.

STOP

14. The next day you go back into work and hand in your case notes on the thirteen-year-old's abuse case you are working on to the secretary for typing. Imagine yourself as that secretary reading this material.

STOP

Please return to the beginning of the paper.

Appendix C
Personal Assumptions

1. Working with offenders involves confronting intense, primitive, complex and often ambivalent feelings, fantasies and inner imagery in practitioners.

2. Acceptance, exploration and discussion of these feelings, fantasies and images both by the individual practitioner and by co-leaders is a pre-condition for successful group work with this population.

3. Repressed and/or unacknowledged feelings either within an individual practitioner or between co-leaders may have a negative impact on offender work.

4. Sexual arousal generated both by the events being discussed by sexual offenders and by processing these events with a co-leader is a "normal" part of offender work. This arousal may include sexual feelings towards a co-leader.

5. The psychological profiles of sexual offender practitioners contain elements that may parallel those of either offenders or victims, e.g., compulsive/obsessive sexual ideation and/or behaviors; victim behavior. If this is true for a particular practitioner, acknowledgment and integration of this profile is both imperative and a potentially invaluable asset to his or her work with this population.

6. Feeling comfortable with and clear about the nature of "healthy sexuality" and the broader concept of "Eros" is an important component of sexual offender work.

7. Sexual-offender treatment practitioners may also have been victims of sexual abuse. If this is the case, work in this field will generally trigger feelings, fantasies and thoughts about this abuse history. Finding a safe place to work through these victim issues is essential both to effective work with clients and to the practitioner's ability or willingness to remain in the sex offender field.

3

Impact on Clinicians: Stressors and Providers of Sex-Offender Treatment

LAWRENCE ELLERBY, M.A.[1]

Although the empirical literature on the assessment and treatment of sex offenders increases, little research into how providing sex offender treatment affects therapists has been done. Given the difficult nature of sex-offender treatment, it may be inevitable that clinicians will be affected by work in this area.

The provision of treatment services, to effect change in others, has an impact on the practitioner (Farber, 1983). As Kottler (1993) states, AThe process of psychotherapy flows in two directions, obviously influencing the client but also affecting the personal life of the clinician. This impact can be for better or for worse, making the helping professions among the most spiritually fulfilling, as well as the most emotionally draining human endeavors" (p. xi).

Understanding how the therapeutic process affects the clinician is extremely important. If mental health service providers are unaware of the effect of their work on themselves, they may be at risk for unhealthy or destructive coping (Norcross & Prochaska, 1986; Thoreson, Miller & Krauskopf, 1989), are likely to be less effective in their attempts at interventions with clients (Deutsch, 1985; Guy, Poelstra, & Stark, 1989), and may experience burnout (Farber & Heifetz, 1982). Awareness of the effects of clinical work on providers is also essential for appropriate training, supervision, job design, support, and self-care for mental health professionals.

Stressors in Clinical Practice

Several areas have been associated with therapist stress, including: 1) the inherent stressors of the therapeutic process and the therapeutic relationship (Farber &

[1] Lawrence Ellerby, M.A., is Clinical Coordinator at the Forensic Behavioral Management Clinic for the Native Clan Organization in Winnepeg, Manitoba, Canada.

Heifetz, 1981); 2) the emotional strain of counseling (Bermak, 1977; Boice & Myers, 1987; Chessick, 1978; Daniels, 1974); 3) clinicians' cognitions, beliefs and expectations about their responsibilities and capabilities (Deutsch, 1984; Farber &Heifetz, 1982); 4) ambiguity in determining treatment progress and outcome (Deutsch, 1984); and 5) operational problems such as excessive workloads and organizational politics (Bermak, 1977). In addition, providing services to "difficult" clients has been identified consistently as a significant source of therapist stress (Hellman, Morrison & Abramowitz, 1987; Chessick, 1978; Daniels, 1974; Farber, 1979; Rogow, 1970). Patient behaviors associated with increased therapist stress cluster into two distinct categories: resistant behaviors and overtly psychopathological symptoms. Farber and Heifetz (1981) and Deutsch (1984) identified patient apathy or lack of motivation as a significant stressor. Strasburger (1986) and Steenson (1987) noted the difficulties associated with providing services to mandated clients who may lack motivation to change and resist external influences. Concerning psychopathology, clinicians have identified patients suffering severe depression, borderline states and narcissistic personalities as among the most stressful to work with (Deutsch, 1984; Hellman, Morrison & Abramowitz, 1987). The most stressful forms of patient behavior identified by therapists have also included making suicidal statements, expressions of aggression and hostility, passive-aggressive behavior, lying, extreme client dependency and clients contacting the therapist at home by telephone. While examining the experience of stress and burnout among social workers providing services to AIDS patients, Egan (1993) found that working with clients who were socially stigmatized served as another factor that may generate stress for clinicians.

Stressors and the Sex-Offender Treatment Provider

Individuals providing treatment services to sex offenders must not only cope with the stresses identified as an intrinsic part of psychotherapy and the counseling profession, but must also contend with the demands of working primarily, if not exclusively, with challenging clients who, for the most part, may exhibit several characteristics identified in the literature as among the most stressful for clinicians.

Sex offenders generally enter treatment involuntarily. Their initial involvement in treatment typically occurs to mitigate consequences (i.e., to reduce the type and/or length of sentences or to secure early release from a correctional institution) or because treatment is mandated. As a result, sex offender therapists must often contend with clients whose involvement in the treatment process may be a means to other ends, rather than as a way to effect personal change. Because of this, sex offenders are likely to present as unmotivated, resistant, deceptive, manipulative, angry, hostile, and controlling. Besides defensive posturing, sex offenders may also present as narcissistic, antisocial, and sexualized in their comments and behaviors, and may possess depressed, suicidal, needy, dependent, and demanding demeanors. These styles of presentation have all been identified with stress among clinicians providing treatment to other populations.

Concerning the target behaviors for change (inappropriate sexual interests and behaviors) sex offenders often deny, minimize, rationalize, justify, and project responsibility for their actions to minimize the seriousness of their offending behavior and/or to avoid culpability. Sex offenders also typically lack a genuine emotional appreciation, or empathy, for the effects of their offenses on their victim/survivors. Experiencing and confronting this lack of acknowledgment of accountability and remorse and empathy may serve as another source of clinicians' stress.

O'Connell, Leberg and Donaldson (1990) report that in working with sex offenders, clinicians commonly find that offenders' problems are more severe than would first appear and that offenders are often unrealistically optimistic about their ability to control their behavior. Discovering that a client's level of pathology, risk, and potential dangerousness are greater than initially believed can serve as a stressor both through dealing with the offender and in determining case and risk management. Furthermore, working with offenders who wrongly believe they are cured or who have an inflated sense of their ability to manage their risk can contribute to therapist stress by the offenders' resistance to further interventions, disregard for interventions (i.e., a willingness to place themselves in high risk situations to test themselves), and the therapist's concern about the risk for reoffending.

Besides facing myriad stressful client characteristics, individuals providing sex-offender treatment are repeatedly exposed to inappropriate and deviant sexual interests and behaviors (both offending and nonoffending), stories of sexualized and nonsexualized violence, accounts of deviant sexual fantasies and arousal, exposure to pornography and to issues related to degradation, dehumanization, control, neglect, and verbal, physical, sexual, and psychological abuse. Abel (1983) stated that clinicians must attend closely to the impact of working daily with rapists. In his view, exploring detailed accounts of violent fantasies and horrific acts can imbue the therapist with awareness of a world of pervasive violence.

The absence of training and supervision for clinicians working with this difficult and at times high-risk client population serves as another potential source of stress. Ellerby, Gutkin, Smith, and Atkinson (1993) in one survey found that, for the most part, therapists lacked offender-specific training before beginning to deliver sex offender treatment. Most therapists (66%) described themselves as poorly or not at all prepared to work with sex offenders. Another 24% saw themselves as only somewhat prepared. The training that clinicians described having received was primarily nonexperiential and included participation in conferences (45%), local workshops (82%), and reading books (90%) and journals (71%). Only 5% of the sex offender practitioners described having received training from a recognized sex-offender treatment program, and only 18% received clinical supervision by a mental health professional with forensic training and/or experience as part of their training. Most of the clinicians surveyed (71%) said that once they began providing sex-offender treatment, their opportunities for further training and continuing education were inadequate. Practitioners also reported concern about a lack of clinical supervision to support them in work with offenders and limited opportunity for professional development. Twenty-nine percent (29%) of the therapists said that they did not receive any supervision. Of those who did have supervision, the number of hours was relatively limited (1 to 2 hours per week), and supervision often took the form of peer supervision or supervision by an administrator, rather than by a clinician. Similar findings were reported by Plyer, Woolley, and Anderson (1990) who found that three-quarters of the respondent clinicians who provided treatment to incest offenders had no offender-specific training, and over half the respondents reported having no continuing training.

Another potential stressor for sex-offender treatment therapists is ambiguity regarding treatment outcomes and efficacy of sex-offender treatment. Because treatment does not "cure" sex-offending behavior and self-monitoring and self-management are lifelong processes (Pithers, Marques, Gibat, & Marlatt, 1983), no definitive conclusion about an offender's recovery is possible. Besides this uncertainty about an offender's capacity to manage risk, clinicians' confidence in the efficacy of sex-offender treatment may be diminished as long-term follow-up shows that recidivism continues to occur 10-31 years after release (Hanson, Steffy, & Gauthier, 1992). Farrenkopf (1992) found in his survey of sex-offender treatment providers that some clinicians over time became more pessimistic about the prospect of client change, with a little over half the respondents reporting diminished hopes and expectations in working with sex offenders.

The reality of sex offenders' reoffending is another stressor with which treatment providers must contend. In this type of intervention, the significance of a return to the target behavior that clinicians attempt to help the offender modify and manage is considerable. The emotional, societal, political, and professional aftermaths of a client's reoffending can potentially be more extensive than treatment failures in other types of clinical practice.

Sex-offender treatment providers may also experience stress because of community and justice system expectations that clinicians are responsible for accurately evaluating and managing risk. In this area, clinicians have the added pressure of acting in a client's best interests, in the interests of the referring agency (e.g., courts, correctional institutions, probation, or parole offices) and the community's best interest. This pressure may be most evident when clinicians must determine the client's reoffense risk and the likelihood of lapsing behaviors such as alcohol use, pornography, and deviant sexual fantasies, as well as decide how such lapses may be managed in the community (e.g., working with a lapse versus returning the offender to prison).

Problems in the systems in which clinicians work are another source of stress. Ryan and Lane (1991) state that treatment providers worry about the system's inability to protect potential victims and its failure to remove dangerous offenders from the community. Thirty-eight percent (38%) of the sex-offender therapists in Farrenkopf's (1992) study reported they were disillusioned with the criminal justice system (e.g., inconsistencies in the justice system, punitive correctional staff attitudes) and discouraged by society's "too little, too late" reactive approach and lack of support for preventive programs.

Clinicians must also live and work in communities in which a stigma is attached to the client group that they serve. Often, only a few individuals understand offender treatment and offer support or appreciation for the importance and difficulty of this work. Ryan and Lane (1991) suggest that sex-offender therapists may feel alienated from their community or workplace, face hostility and/or emotionally volatile conflicts with clinicians who treat victims, and find their belief in treatment challenged or belittled by colleagues. Ellerby et al. (1993) found that, among the clinicians surveyed, 68% reported discomfort with telling people that they work with sex offenders, 71% felt the need to justify the work, and 90% reported incidences of negative responses from others about their sex-offender specialization. Only 47% of the therapists reported positive reactions to their work.

Given the range and type of stressors involved in working with sex offenders, it is understandable why Scott (1989) suggests that psychotherapy with criminals is the most demanding work in the entire mental-health field.

The Effects of Providing Sex-Offender Treatment

Although the literature identifies the stressors associated with clinical practice, much of which is relevant to sex-offender clinicians, there is less research addressing the impact of these various stressors on therapists. Although research into the occurrence of burnout in mental health professionals has been done, the nature of stressors that contribute to burnout has merited less attention. Some preliminary studies of the effects of sex-offender treatment on providers suggest that providing service to sex offenders affects clinicians' personal and professional lives in several ways.

Emotional Impact

Given the stressors associated with clinical practice, the difficult nature of sex offenders as clients, and the likely impact of constant and repeated exposure to various forms of abuse, violence and dysfunction, an emotional toll on clinicians is not surprising. Evidence suggests that, as a function of this work, changes occur in how therapists experience and express feelings.

Farrenkopf (1992) found that many sex-offender therapists in his sample reported decreased sensitivity or dulling of their emotions. Therapists described an increase in feelings of anger and frustration, development of a cynical outlook, and a decrease in sense of humor. They also reported becoming more confrontational and less tolerant of others' behavior than before beginning such work. Fewer clinicians reported an increased sensitivity toward others and more empathy for human suffering. In addition, clinicians reported experiencing these changes not only in their contacts with clients but also in their personal and social interactions. A quarter of the clinicians in that study reported feelings of generalized high stress, exhaustion, depression, or burnout, sometimes leading to leaving the sex-offender treatment specialization. Ellerby et al. (1993) also found sex-offender treatment practitioners reporting that they found themselves to be more pessimistic, cynical, and angry. However, in this study, more than half the therapists described becoming more empathic and compassionate.

Boundary and Safety Issues

Boundary issues are significant among sex-offender treatment providers, particularly female therapists. Ellerby et al. (1993) found that most of the female therapists (84%) described feeling their personal boundaries had been invaded by clients, and 42% described feeling sexualized by offenders. Male therapists reported feeling these invasions much less frequently (34% and 16% respectively). Many therapists (58%) of both genders identified having felt unclean after a session with a sex offender.

Sex-offender treatment providers report concerns about safety issues. Therapists were concerned about their personal safety with sex offenders in their case load, had become more cautious in their personal relationships, and generally felt more unsafe. Ellerby et al. (1993) found that many female (79%) and male (63%) clinicians reported having felt threatened or endangered by a client. Farrenkopf (1992) noted that female clinicians were particularly prone to feeling increased vulnerability or threat of abuse and more concerned about personal safety and their children's safety. They reported becoming vigilant in their daily lives.

Similarly, Ellerby et al. (1993) found that female therapists reported feeling more vulnerable, fearful, and cautious, were more concerned about their safety in personal relationships and described being hypervigilant around others and more protective of their own or their family's safety. Ryan and Lane (1991) also described clinicians who work with sex offenders as oversensitive to dangerous situations and becoming overprotective of children and other loved ones. Ellerby et al. (1993) further report that both female and male clinicians described becoming more protective of their children, extremely aware of how others interact with their children, and more fearful for their children's safety. Clinicians suggested that since they began working with sex offenders, they have become more open about discussing sexuality and sexual abuse with their children and monitored their children's exposure to the media (e.g., television and movies) more closely. They also report becoming more cautious in parenting than before doing such work.

Responses to Sex Offenders and Deviant Sexual Behavior

In response to repeated exposure to a range of deviant sexual behaviors and fantasies, clinicians' perceptions of their clients, the severity of their clients' offending behavior and the risk a client may present may be distorted. Ellerby et al. (1993) found that many clinicians acknowledged having felt at some time desensitized to deviant sexual behavior. This desensitization has the potential negatively to affect the clinician's ability to assess risk and to provide the most appropriate intervention. Ryan and Lane (1991) suggest that it is common among clinicians working with sex offenders to develop ambivalent emotions about the client and his or her behavior, to experience victim or aggressor identification, and to accept offenders' minimizations and rationalizations.

Sexuality

Given that sex-offender clinicians are immersed in the exposure to deviant sexuality, the clinicians' sexuality may be affected. Garrison (1992) suggests that working with sex offenders may affect the worker's personal life, specifically the clinician's sexuality. He reported statements such as "I feel sexually numb — neutral," and "I have lost interest in sex," and "Sex is a nightmare," as "typical comments" from colleagues who work with sex offenders (quoted in Cooper, 1994, p. 3). Farrenkopf (1992) reported that some clinicians described a reduction in their sexual behavior, while others said that they had become more considerate of their partners sexually. Ellerby et al. (1993) found that male and female therapists reported experiencing a reduced interest in sex (26% and 37%, respectively) and a reduction in sexual behavior (37% and 32%, respectively). Male and female clinicians also reported that, as a direct result of exposure to deviant sexuality at work, they: 1) have avoided a sexual contact (37% and 58%, respectively); 2) have been distracted during a sexual contact (32% and 53%, respectively); and 3) prematurely ended a sexual contact (21% and 32%, respectively). Clinicians also described questioning their past sexual behavior (males 68%, females 53%) and the appropriateness of their current sexual behavior (males 37%, females 21%). Ryan and Lane (1991) suggest that ultimately this work forces all interventionists to question the normality of their own sexuality, sexual fantasies and sexual experiences.

Ellerby et al. (1993) also found that some therapists experienced sexual thoughts, fantasies and feelings toward offenders. A few clinicians acknowledged having had a sexual dream about a client (females 5%, males 11%) and 11% of both female and male clinicians had experienced sexual fantasies about a client. Although none of the male therapists reported being sexually attracted to a client, 16% of the female clinicians described experiencing sexual feelings toward a client. Given the frequent sexual content of this work, it is not surprising that some descriptions of sexual behavior could be sexually arousing to clinicians. In the same study 32% of the male therapists and 21% of the female therapists acknowledged having become sexually aroused in response to offenders' descriptions of their *nonoffending* sexual history. Many therapists reported experiencing sexual arousal to offenders' accounts of their deviant and sexual offending behaviors (males 42%, females 16%). This finding is particularly significant given that so many clinicians report that they do not have adequate training and supervisory supports that may help them to address such concerns.

Ellerby et al. (1993) also found that both male and female therapists who conducted sex-offender groups reported experiencing a high frequency of sexual thoughts and fantasies about their opposite-gender group co-facilitator. Approximately one-quarter of the therapists acknowledged becoming sexually involved with a co-facilitator.

The Effects of Recidivism

Ellerby et al. (1993) identified a range of feelings among clinicians after clients reoffend. Therapists reported feeling angry (84%), disillusioned and depressed (79%), doubtful about their competence (74%), inadequate (58%), and guilty (42%). Clearly, a tendency toward personalizing an offender's relapse has a profound impact on the clinician. Some clinicians can cope with such instances by reviewing their involvement in a specific case and attempting to learn from the experience. In other instances, however, personalizing the relapse can traumatize the mental health professional and may impede his or her ability to work with this population or may lead to ending work in sex-offender treatment.

Future Directions

Sex-offender treatment is a field in which practitioners face several significant stressors that directly affect their personal and professional lives. Given the growing need for such treatment services, we must develop a greater understanding than we currently have of the effects of this work on clinicians. Then the appropriate training, supervision, and supports may be established to prepare individuals for it as they continue to provide services to this difficult client group.

To date, research in this area is limited. Although some studies postulate the potential effects of sex-offender treatment on clinicians and unanimously find that working with sex offenders differs in important ways from work with other client populations, this is primarily a nonresearch literature. The existing research must be considered preliminary because it is based on small samples. Replicating the initial investigations with larger samples will be important. In addition, the research to date has focused exclusively on specialists in sex-offender treatment. Future research should begin to examine whether the stressors and effects reported by sex-offender therapists are unique to those practitioners, or if parallels exist among clinicians who provide services to sexual-abuse survivors or among mental-health professionals who do not specialize in sexual abuse or sex-offending areas.

In summary, attempting to assess and manage the risk of sexual offenders is a significant contribution toward community protection. Clinicians who take on the challenge of this work must be supported in the most appropriate manner possible to help them to maintain their own mental and physical health.

References

Abel, G. (1983). Preventing men from becoming rapists. In G.S. Albee and H. Leltenberg (Eds.), *Promoting sexual responsibility and preventing sexual problems*. Hanover, NH: University Press of New England.

Bermak, G. (1977). Do psychiatrists have special emotional problems? *American Journal of Psychoanalysis, 37,* 141-146.

Boice, R., & Myers, P.E. (1987). Which setting is healthier and happier, academe or private practice? *Professional Psychology: Research and Practice, 18,* 526-529.

Chessick, R.D. (1978). The sad soul of the psychiatrist. *Bulletin of the Menninger Clinic, 42,* 1-9.

Cooper, M. (1994). Working with sex offenders. *In Setting standards and guiding principles for the assessment, treatment, and management of sex offenders in British Columbia* Vancouver, BC: British Columbia Institute on the Family.

Daniels, A.K. (1974). What troubles trouble shooters. In P.M. Roman & H.M. Trice (Eds.), *The sociology of psychotherapy.* New York: Aronson.

Deutsch, C.J. (1984). Self-reported sources of stress among psychotherapists. *Professional Psychology: Research and Practice, 15,* 833-845.

Deutsch, C.J. (1985). A survey of therapists' personal problems and treatment. *Professional Psychology: Research and Practice, 16,* 305-315.

Egan, M. (1993). Resilience at the front lines: Hospital social work with AIDS patients and burnout. *Social Work in Health Care, 18,* 109-123

Ellerby, L., Gutkin, B., Smith, T., & Atkinson, R. (1993). *Treating sex offenders: The impact on clinicians.* Poster Presentation, 12th Annual Conference of the Association for the Treatment of Sexual Abusers, Boston, Massachusetts.

Farber, B. (1979). The effects of psychotherapeutic practice upon psychotherapists: A phenomenological investigation. *Dissertation Abstracts International, 40,* 447B.

Farber, B. (1983). The effects of psychotherapeutic practice upon psychotherapists. *Psychotherapy: Theory, Research and Practice, 20,* 174-182.

Farber, B., & Heifetz L.J. (1981). The satisfactions and stresses of psychotherapeutic work: A factor analytic study. *Professional Psychology, 12,* 621-629.

Farber, B., & Heifetz L.J. (1982). The process and dimension of burnout in psychotherapists. *Professional Psychology, 13,* 293-301.

Farrenkopf, T. (1992). What happens to therapists who work with sex offenders? *Journal of Offender Rehabilitation, 16,* 217-223.

Garrison, K. (1992). *Working with sex offenders: A practice guide.* Norwich, England: Social Work Monographs, University of East Anglia.

Guy, J.D., Poelstra, P.L., & Stark, M.J. (1989). Personal distress and therapeutic effectiveness: National survey of psychologists practicing psychotherapy. *Professional Psychology: Research and Practice, 20,* 48-50.

Hanson, R.K., Steffy, R.A., & Gauthier, R. (1992). Long-term follow up of child molesters: Risk predictors and treatment outcome. Report prepared for Ministry of the Solicitor General of Canada: Corrections Branch.

Hellman, I.D., Morrison, T.L., & Abramowitz, S.I. (1987). Therapist flexibility/rigidity and work stress. *Professional Psychology: Research and Practice, 18*, 21-27.

Kottler, J. A. (1993). *On being a therapist.* San Francisco: Jossey-Bass.

Norcross, J.C., & Prochaska, J.O. (1986). Psychotherapist heal thyself: The psychological distress and self change of psychologists, counselors and laypersons. *Psychotherapy, 23*, 102-114.

O'Connell, M.A., Leberg, E., & Donaldson, C.R. (1990). *Working with sex offenders: guidelines for therapist selection.* Newbury Park, CA: Sage.

Pithers, W.D., Marques, J.K., Gibat, C.C., & Marlatt, G.A. (1983). Relapse prevention with sexual aggressives: A self-control model of treatment and the maintenance of change. In J.G. Greer & I.R. Stuart (Eds.), *The sexual aggressor: Current perspectives on treatment,* (pp. 292-310). New York: Guilford.

Plyer, A., Woolley, C. S., & Anderson, T. K. (1990). Current treatment providers. In A.L. Horton, B.L. Johnson, L.M. Roundy, & D. Williams (Eds.), *The incest perpetrator: A family member no once wants to treat,* (pp. 198-218) Newbury Park, CA: Sage.

Rogow, A. (1970). *The psychiatrists.* New York: Putnam.

Ryan, G. D., & Lane, S. L. (1991). The impact of sexual abuse on the interventionist. In G.D. Ryan & S.L. Lane (Eds.), *Juvenile sexual offending: Causes, consequences and corrections,* 411-428. Toronto: Lexington Books.

Scott, E. (1989). Is there a criminal mind? *International Journal of Offender Therapy and Comparative Criminology, 33*, 215-226.

Steenson, N. (1987). A comparison of the stresses generated for mental health practitioners working with mandated and voluntary clients in agency setting and in private practice. Unpublished doctoral dissertation. Pacific University, Forest Grove, OR.

Strasburger, L. (1986). The treatment of antisocial syndromes: Therapists' feelings. In Reid, W. (Ed.) *Unmasking the Psychopath,* pp. 191-206. New York: W.W. Norton.

Thoreson, R.W., Miller, M., & Krauskopf, C.J. (1989). The distressed psychologist: Prevalence and treatment considerations. *Professional Psychology: Research and Practice, 20*, 153-158.

4

Working with Sex Offenders: The Impact on Practitioners

K. E. JACKSON, Ph.D.,[1]
CYNTHIA HOLZMAN, M.A.,[2]
TIMOTHY BARNARD, M.A.,[3] &
CHERYL PARADIS, Psy.D.[4]

T his study identifies aspects of the professional and personal impact of working with sexual offenders on practitioners. Literature devoted to the study of sex-offender assessment, etiology, and treatment is increasing, but little research is being done on the impact of this work on practitioners.

Literature Review

Professional "burnout" has emerged as a phenomenon among clinicians who work with difficult populations. Practitioners have become aware of the potential negative effects of their work. Such effects include experiencing: 1) depression; 2) stress-related physical disorders; 3) diminished interest in the profession; 4) loss of compassion; or 5) cynicism (Freudenberger & Robbins, 1979, cited in McCann & Pearlman, 1990). Researchers identify trauma survivors as a specific client population that presents unique challenges to practitioners (McCann & Pearlman, 1990).

Sex offenders may be seen as persons with severe personality disorders, many of whom have also been victims themselves. Strasburger (1986) discusses the impact of working with antisocial personality-disordered patients: "Countertransference often undermines the staff's feelings of competence and self-respect, adding to the phenomenon known as burn-out." (p. 196). Strasburger identifies several specific countertransferential reactions that may be experienced by practi-

[1] K.E. Jackson, Ph.D., is affiliated with the Metropolitan Center, 80 East 11th St., New York, NY 10003. The authors would like to thank Reuben Margolis, Ph.D., of S.U.N.Y. Downstate for statistical assistance, and Samuel D. Johnson, Ph.D., of Baruch College for technical and editorial assistance.
[2] Cynthia Holzman, M.A., is affiliated with the Carrier Foundation in Belle Mead, NJ 08502.
[3] Timothy Barnard, M.A., is affiliated with the Adult Diagnostic and Treatment Center in Avenel, NJ 07001.
[4] Cheryl Paradis, Psy.D., is affiliated with the S.U.N.Y. Downstate Medical Center in Brooklyn, NY.

tioners, including: 1) fear of assault or harm; 2) feelings of helplessness and guilt; 3) feelings of invalidity; 4) loss of identity; 5) denial; 6) hatred; or 7) rage.

McCann and Pearlman (1990) note two ways to characterize the impact of working with trauma on professionals. The literature about professional burnout suggests that the situational factors of the trauma determine the impact on the practitioner. The literature regarding countertransference, on the other hand, suggests that the therapist's own unresolved psychological conflicts determine her or his reactions to traumatic material. McCann and Pearlman (1990) offer an interactive approach that synthesizes intrapsychic and situational factors. "Our notion of vicarious traumatization is somewhat broader than countertransference, as it implies that much of the therapist's cognitive world will be altered by hearing traumatic client material . . . Whether these changes are ultimately destructive to the helper and to the therapeutic process depends, in large part, on the extent to which the therapist is able to engage in a parallel process to that of the victim client, the process of integrating and transforming these experiences of horror or violation" (p. 136).

Further, McCann and Pearlman maintain, "Although the burnout literature is relevant to working with trauma victims, we concur with others . . . that the potential effects of working with trauma survivors are distinct from those of working with other difficult populations because the therapist is exposed to the emotionally shocking images of horror and suffering that are characteristic of serious traumas" (1990, p. 134). Work with sexual offenders increases the complexity of these effects, however. Sex-offender therapists are exposed both to the suffering clients endured as victims and to the suffering offenders then inflicted as perpetrators.

Distinct and identifiable difficulties are posed for the practitioner working with antisocial, personality-disordered clients. Farrenkopf (1992) explores the impact of sex offender treatment on therapists in terms of how specific client characteristics infringe on therapists. He identifies the following qualities as particularly problematic traits of sex offenders: 1) irresponsibility; 2) narcissistic personality structure; and 3) the lack of motivation for change. Respondents in Farrenkopf's study identify ways therapists are affected by these traits in treatment. Farrenkopf further identifies four phases of adjustment therapists may experience as they come to terms with their work with offenders: 1) shock; 2) a sense of mission; 3) emergence of repressed emotions, usually anger; and 4) either "erosion" or "adaptation." "Erosion" refers to an escalation of feelings experienced in the anger phase, but also includes exhaustion, depression, resentment, and thoughts about treatment futility. Alternatively, "adaptation" refers to a more successful way of coping: 1) adopting a detached attitude; 2) lowering expectations; and 3) coming to terms with "the human dark side" (Farrenkopf, 1992, p. 221). Other reactions include a heightened sense of vulnerability and vigilance (particularly among female therapists), frustration with the criminal justice system or society, and emotional "hardening."

Our interest in the ways practitioners may be affected by this work derived from our own experiences and observations of colleagues. We saw a wide range of burnout reactions and styles of coping with problems presented by working with this difficult population. Reactions to the work were not related to clinicians' years of experience, training, or gender. The more we looked, the less we understood. That is, we found no direct connections among how colleagues experienced the work or its impact on themselves, and their effectiveness as therapists, or their education or enthusiasm for the work. When we began to survey clinicians about how they managed the relationships between their personal lives and their work, the confusion increased. For example, several therapists who had worked with offenders for more than ten years said they no longer discussed the work with their spouses, but others found supportive discussions with family members invaluable and essential to their effectiveness. Not all practitioners appeared to be affected by their work in the same ways. Therefore, we did not assume that therapists had any particular or specific reaction to this work. Instead, we sought to identify the spectrum of psychological and behavioral responses to working with sex offenders.

Method

Subjects

The sample for this study is drawn from the international Association for the Treatment of Sexual Abusers (ATSA) roster for the 1993 conference. Questionnaires were sent through the mail to all ATSA members residing in the United States, yielding 332 possible respondents. We included self-addressed stamped envelopes for return of the questionnaire. From the initial mailing, 107 responses were received, and of those, 98 questionnaires yielded usable responses.

Materials

The questionnaire was a 53-item survey designed to allow respondents to describe their experiences and reactions to working with sex offenders through both short-answer and forced-choice questions.

Procedure

The procedure for this study was a mixed method, using both qualitative and quantitative approaches. Questions for this survey were drawn from both the existing literature and from discussions with colleagues. Subjects were asked to describe reactions to a variety of questions briefly and were assured anonymity. Because this is exploratory research, the survey questions are primarily open-ended.

Using random selection of a subset of questionnaires (12), a content analysis was done. Three of the researchers collaborated on this task until consensus regarding categories was achieved. After developing a coding scheme, responses were quantified, and the results were transferred to bubble-coding sheets for computerized data analysis.

Results

Demographic Data

Respondents ranged from 21 to more than 60 years of age. More than half our respondents were between the ages of 41 and 50 (53%), with the next largest group 51 to 60 years of age (28%). Most respondents were male (75%).

The respondents reported a range of years of experience as psychological practitioners. Forty-seven percent (47%) of respondents reported having more than 16 years' experience (not limited to work with offenders).

Respondents' Years of Experience

0-5 years	12%
6-10 years	24%
11-15 years	18%
16-20 years	27%
21+ years	20%

Most of the respondents reported between zero and 10 years' experience working with offenders and victims. The largest group of respondents report working with offenders between 6 and 10 years (41%), with the next largest group working with offenders between zero and 5 years (24%). Thirty-seven per-cent (37%) of practitioners working with victims reported between 1 year's and 5 years' experience, and 34% reported between 6 and 10 years' experience.

Approximately half the respondents said they were working with offend-ers between 16 and 26 or more hours per week (56%). Respondents reported working with victims for 10 hours or fewer per week (82%)

More than one-third (38%) of the respondents had earned Master's de-grees. The respondents' reports of their educational degrees is as follows:

Master's degree	38%
Master's in Social Work	28%
Ed.D., Psy.D. , Ph.D.	31%
Other	3%

Respondents identified many forms of training that prepare practitioners for working with sexual offenders. The most prevalent form of preparatory train-ing is participation in workshops and seminars (83%); the second most prevalent form is research/literature (65%); the most prevalent third form is supervision (50%); the fourth is an internship (44%); the fifth form cited is on-the-job training (30%). The majority (81%) of respondents reported multiple preparatory training experiences. Overwhelmingly, respondents reported adequate training for their work with sex offenders (84%).

The most common work setting reported by respondents was private practice (70%), followed by correctional facilities, including residential centers (28%), and mental health clinics (27%). Some respondent practitioners worked in hospital settings (21% outpatient; 13% inpatient).

Most respondents (93%) reported working with an adult-client population; 68% also reported working with adolescents.

Treatment Delivery

Most respondents (96%) reported using more than one treatment modality (individual, group, marital, and family). The two most prevalent modalities in use were reported to be individual therapy and group therapy. Nearly three-quarters of the practitioners reported using confrontation (74%); fewer respondents indicated using psychoeducational techniques (43%) as the single most commonly employed technique. However, when respondents were asked to identify whether they employed more than one type of treatment, 83% indicated using multiple types. Of these, 91% identified using psychoeducational techniques as adjunctive to another form of treatment.

The theoretical orientation most commonly identified was cognitive-behavioral (60%). Other orientations were less prevalent among respondents. However, a large minority of respondents (22%) identified more than one theoretical orientation (including psychodynamic, family systems, eclectic).

Practitioners identified several ways of measuring therapeutic success. The most common (54%) was the recidivism rate, and the least common indications (12%) came through responses from an offender's family.

Respondents most frequently identified their own therapeutic skills or use of particular therapeutic modalities as the key to their own effectiveness as practitioners. The least common factor in success was reported to be the use of supervision and support (3%).

Personal and Professional Impact of Work

One area of impact on practitioners is visual imagery about sexual violence. Many practitioners (67%) reported experiencing visual images of sexual assaults committed by clients. Practitioners identified the following reactions to these images: painful and disturbing (21%), repulsive (19%), and/or arousing (1%). Some practitioners reported experiencing a combination of these reactions (28%). Half the sample (51%) reported that clients' detailed descriptions of offending behavior trigger their own sexual fantasies. While 41% of respondents revealed experiencing sexual fantasies about clients, only 29% identified those visual images as intrusive.

Another dimension of impact includes respondents' views of the criminal justice system. Most respondents (77%) reported changes in their views of the criminal justice system. Only a small percentage (4%) regarded the criminal justice system as more effective than they previously believed. Conversely, most reported seeing the criminal justice system as less effective than they saw it before working with offenders (62%), and some respondents indicated other changes in their perceptions of the system (13%).

Behavioral changes attributed to work with offenders

Very few respondents indicated any increases in drug (1%) or alcohol (8%) use because of working with offenders. Conversely, small percentages of respondents reported a decrease in drug use (5%), or alcohol intake (6%). Some respondents reported experiencing changes in appetite (11%). A more substantial percentage of the sample identified changes in sleep patterns attributed to their work (30%).

Almost half the respondents (48%) identified changes in their own sexual behavior since working with offenders. Most of those respondents revealed a decrease in interest/activity (27%), and a very small percentage reported an increase in their interest/activity (4%). Other respondents identified other changes in sexual behavior (17%).

Over half (57%) of the sample reported changing their own behavior around children because of their work. Differentiating behavior from affect, a slightly larger percentage (59%) reported experiencing heightened anxiety regarding the safety of their own children or grandchildren. An even greater percentage reported that they have become more vigilant around strangers (65%).

Many respondents (54%) expressed fear for their own safety. Most respondents reported being assaulted (verbally and/or physically) by clients (51%). A smaller group reported that they fear possible retribution from clients (42%). Over a quarter of the respondents (27%) identified inadequate security in their workplace as the source of their concerns about safety.

Among respondents who reported being assaulted by clients, the majority reported experiencing verbal assault (51%), and a much smaller percentage reported physical assaults without verbal aggression (8%). Despite concerns regarding safety, most respondents reported that they intend to continue working with offenders (95%).

Coping strategies

Respondents reported using several methods to cope with the effects of their work and reported that supervision is the most common strategy used to address personal and professional impacts of working with offenders. Most respondents (79%) reported receiving supervision on a weekly, monthly, or as-needed basis. Respondents reported seeking supervision at least as frequently (46%), if not more frequently (33%) than before they began work with sexual offenders. Only a small percentage (8%) reported seeking supervision less frequently since they began to work with offenders. Most respondents identified supervision as helpful (88%).

Respondents reported three primary benefits of supervision: 1) validation of the therapist's perceptions and/or other perceptions (48%); 2) case management (27%); and 3) the release of feelings (15%). A relatively small percentage of respondents (24%) identified multiple benefits from supervision.

Many respondents (43%) entered therapy for themselves since beginning work with offenders. Another way some respondents reported handling the impact of their work is to avoid discussing it with others for a variety of reasons. Some respondents believed others would not understand (31%); some were tired of talking about it (9%); some reported concern about patient confidentiality (5%); and some practitioners reported multiple reasons to avoid discussing the work (12%). The largest percentage of respondents (40%) indicated they avoid discussing work, but did not identify specific reasons.

Nearly a third (31%) of the sample identified separation of work and personal life as a coping mechanism. To a much smaller extent, 4% of the sample reported adopting an increasingly detached attitude. Respondents reported other ways to manage including: pursuing recreational activities, hobbies and vacations (20%), or engaging in exercise and sports (16%). Other ways to cope also were reported to involve interpersonal interactions. By far, the most frequently reported form of coping involved receiving support from other sex-offender therapists (88%). To a lesser extent, practitioners identified support from family, friends, or representatives of the criminal justice system as helpful (20%). Not surprisingly, respondents identified a range of other ways to cope not identified above (39%) and using multiple strategies to deal with the effects of their work (40%).

Thoughts about sexual violence

Finally, many respondents indicated that their thoughts about sexual violence had changed since they began to work with sex offenders. Many practitioners replied positively that they had changed their thinking about sexual violence but did not identify the nature of those changes (34%). The most frequently identified change is an increased awareness of the prevalence of sexual violence (31%). A smaller group identified a deepened awareness of offenders' pathology (18%). A few respondents mentioned awareness of the impact of sexual aggression on victims (10%). Surprisingly, only 6% of the sample reported developing a stronger belief in treatment from work with offenders, and 3% of respondents reported frustration with the criminal justice system when asked about sexual violence and personal changes resulting from the work.

Some respondents (29%) reported other changes in their thinking about sexual violence that they attribute to work with offenders. A smaller percentage (23%) reported multiple changes in their thinking resulting from such work.

That change is, possibly, why so many therapists use visualization as a technique. When working with victims, visualization may emerge naturally, but when working with offenders, it is more of a conscious strategy for understanding the perpetrator. His or her inability to identify with the victim is exactly the blockage against which therapists work.

Discussion

Background

This study provoked strong interest and involvement from respondents, as suggested by the high response rate and the thoughtful, detailed responses to difficult, open-ended questions. The responses contained much more information than was coded because our purpose in this phase of the project was strictly descriptive. The next phase will involve exploration of relationships among the variables identified at this stage of our research.

Most respondents are middle-aged men working with adult clients in private practice; however, many respondents work with sex offenders in more than one setting. Practitioners have to work effectively in myriad settings with different treatment modalities. Responses to our questions show a trend toward a cognitive-behavioral treatment orientation; many practitioners use a psycho-educational approach flavored by confrontation. Our respondents are generally practitioners who began work with offenders after gaining experience with other populations. While most respondents have been practicing treatment for more than 16 years, most of the respondents have been working with offenders for fewer than ten years.

We wanted to explore the practitioners' preparatory experiences to understand whether solid theoretical and supervised practical training helped practitioners feel more confident about their work than those without such preparation. We find that virtually none of the respondents identified academic experiences as central. Only one respondent identified specific graduate courses as a source of preparatory training. Another respondent lists "formal academic program," and a third respondent lists "education," which could refer to graduate course work. Nevertheless, these findings point to the relative paucity of training in sex-offender-specific treatment at the graduate level. Instead, respondents report workshops and seminars as their primary training experiences. Given the lack of formal academic training (i.e., course work), it is not surprising that many practitioners express a sense of urgency in their pursuit of knowledge regarding sex-offender treatment and report actively seeking diverse sources of information and training.[5] Some practitioners may have arranged their own practical training experiences in sex offender treatment through development of internship experiences.

Respondents discuss the importance of multifaceted training experiences. Thirty percent (30%) of respondents identify "on-the-job" training as an

---

[5] Some respondents comment on this aspect of preparation: "Never enough," "There is no training available that I'm aware of that adequately prepares one going in. Since starting, I have sought out and received excellent training."

important source of preparation. One respondent comments, "No person should enter this field without close supervision and treatment for their own issues. One college course will not prepare a person for this. Certification should be required and come at the end of much on-the-job training."

Personal and Professional Impact

In conducting this project, one interest involved investigating the sources of therapeutic efficacy. When developing our questions, we conducted a pilot study given to institutional colleagues. They had reported feeling beleaguered, overwhelmed, and exhausted. We asked them, therefore, how and why they could continue working with offenders, despite the frustrations they encountered. These questions seemed particularly important because most offenders do not participate voluntarily, which requires different criteria to determine therapeutic success from those for voluntary participants, such as self-reported satisfaction with therapy, the most common criterion for success in voluntary participation in therapy. With the lack of standardized testing, it appears that practitioners have resolved the question of evaluating therapeutic success in terms of recidivism, an objective, behavioral measure.

We find it somewhat surprising that respondents infrequently identify formal assessment as a measure of therapeutic success. On one hand, recidivism represents a clear, "bottom-line" approach favored by respondents as the primary measure of therapeutic success. On the other hand, recidivism alone is not a gratifying criterion for practitioners. That is, clinicians may find no immediate gratification in work with involuntary patients, as clinicians often do with voluntary clients. Gratification must be delayed until the completion of therapy, and indeed, for as long as follow-up is stipulated. This circumstance seems to affect a practitioner's outlook. Results are so equivocal that practitioners may question their original purpose in treating offenders, especially when there are no objective measures with which to identify mandated clients as successful or failed other than additional incidents of sex offenses.

Why, therefore, do therapists continue to work with offenders? Given the nature of the clients, and the substantial problems their characteristics pose for practitioners (denial, obnoxious behavior, tendencies toward hostile and assaultive behavior, and dependence), the level of respondents' reported commitment to continue the work is surprising. Practitioners reveal a sense of mission, along with awareness of the dire consequences of treatment failure. Some respondents believe that they help victims by working with offenders, are able to witness positive changes, growth and healing among clients, and have a larger sense of purpose despite the daily difficulties of working with offenders. For example, one respondent writes, "I feel in many ways privileged to work with these men (the ones who are remorseful and motivated to change). Some I have learned a great deal from. I have learned to live with paradox — I feel more vulnerable in this world filled with violence, yet I have more hope . . . to see the good qualities in some of these men emerge, to see them care for each other and their families, to see them and their victims' families grow and heal provides great hope and joy for me. . . ."

Although a sense of hope is a powerful motivator, respondents identify a sense of purpose and direction in their work, their own therapeutic skills, and/or use of particular treatment modalities as central in experiencing efficacy. This gratification can be especially important when the work is difficult, or when there is little concrete support from others and great resistance from patients, their lawyers, and other professionals.

Along with our need to feel effective and productive in our work are the other effects, positive and negative, that this work has on our lives. For some clinicians, one negative effect may involve experiences of unwanted visual images. We know that sex offenders may be powerfully affected by visual images. Perhaps the large percentage of practitioners who report experiencing visual images related to their work reflects this. Most respondents in our study report this phenomenon, and a significant percentage find it intrusive and uncomfortable. Such experiences may be similar to processes that McCann and Pearlman (1990) identify as vicarious traumatization. Many therapists feel the need to separate their personal and professional lives and identify doing so as a coping strategy. Nevertheless, we believe that visual images about clients outside the consultation room or supervision may be particularly disturbing to therapists. The recurrence of images also could be experienced as similar to the loss of control that victims endure because of victimization. We may not necessarily want to admit that offenders "get inside" our mental lives, but for some of us, they clearly do.

On the other hand, another respondent group reports that such experiences with images are not disturbing, suggesting that some practitioners use imagery as a therapeutic tool to aid in understanding the offender more clearly than otherwise may be possible. Another possibility is that those therapists perhaps can separate or detach effectively from their work so that such images are less troubling to them than to other clinicians.

We are surprised by the large number of practitioners who have sexual fantasies about their offending clients. We did not ask about the nature of the fantasies. That omission leaves open the question of whether the practitioners have fantasies about direct involvement with clients, clients' behavior with victims, or consensual sexual behavior with clients. Furthermore, we did not specify whether the fantasies were about offenders or victims, and client gender was not stipulated. We also did not ask about practitioners' sexual orientation. Therefore, we do not know whether the fantasies are sexually arousing and/or problematic for therapists.

Another significant concern in this field is the relatively high rate of assaultive behavior by sex offenders toward therapists, including verbal and physical aggression. A quarter of respondents identifies inadequate security as a source of concern about their own safety. Some respondents are concerned about their own safety, but an even greater number fear retribution from clients. Given the many practitioners in private practice settings, these findings reflect a realistic fear about practitioner vulnerability.

Most practitioners report becoming disenchanted with the criminal justice system when working with offenders, viewing it as less effective than they did when they began work with sex offenders. Only some respondents view the criminal justice system as more effective than they earlier perceived, because of the work. This perspective may reflect a sense of helplessness or powerlessness. Some respondents report feeling unsupported or even directly opposed by other sectors of the system, suggesting that occasionally, practitioners experience themselves as beleaguered even by those purporting to be on the same side.

When asking respondents about behavioral changes that they may attribute to their work with offenders, we assumed that respondents differentiated work-related stressors from other stressors. Respondents possibly attribute some behavioral changes to their offender work that could realistically be attributed to outside stressors. However, the results suggest that practitioners perceive the impact of working with offenders to be substantial, and that the forms such impact takes may be identified as specific behavioral changes.

A large proportion of the sample reports changes in sleep patterns attributable to their work. Such changes may be due to intrusive images or unconscious sequelae that do not manifest themselves during waking hours. Another possibility is that sleep-pattern changes reflect a residue from daily activities.

Almost half the respondents attribute changes in their own sexual behavior to their work with sex offenders. The behavioral changes reported vary from a decreased interest in any sexual activity to changes in their approach to sexual encounters. These changes include greater sensitivity to their partners, with particular references to carefully checking their partners' interest in and comfort levels with sex. Practitioners seem to attempt to differentiate themselves from their offender clients, and that differentiation is heightened in the sexual arena. At the other end of the spectrum, some respondents report increased interest in and/or participation in sexual activity. For example, one respondent identifies his own sexual behavior as "predatory," drawing a parallel between his offender clients and himself. Such a report may suggest that some practitioners may become so sensitized to sexual aggression that they question even "normal" sexual behavior.

Practitioners in this study report few changes in drug or alcohol use attributable to working with sex offenders. Clinicians say that they find their work stressful, so it is particularly noteworthy that increased drug and alcohol use is not reported. Our questions do not explore the issue of whether the practitioners abused drugs or alcohol at the beginning of their work with offenders. Instead, our questions are directed at changes experienced in substance use attributable to work with sex offenders. It may be possible to conceptualize substance use as either symptomatic or as a coping strategy.

Another significant behavioral change among clinicians working with sex offenders involves practitioners' behavior around children. Some respondents report concerns that children feel safe and comfortable, with a clear sense of personal boundaries. Other respondents note a tendency to distance themselves from children to protect themselves from possible accusations of inappropriate behavior. Another group of respondents does not identify any specific behavioral changes, but reports increased awareness of the potential for abuse or misunderstanding of innocent behavior. An even greater number of practitioners say that they experience the need for vigilance around strangers.

We identify the tendency to avoid talking about our work to others as professional vigilance. Perhaps clinicians who work with sex offenders experience a heightened sensitivity to social reactions about the nature of the work. The respondents who specify reasons for this avoidance believe that other people will not understand the nature of the work. Two respondents comment: "In the past, before it became a recognized specialty, I had concerns about the reactions of others," and "They may become voyeuristic." Still others appear to avoid discussing their work because that precludes the separation between work and personal lives that most practitioners find essential. We are speculating about practitioners' reasons for avoiding discussion about their work with others; most respondents do not delineate their reasons.

Nearly one-third of the respondents identify separation of work and personal lives as a way to cope with the stress of the work. However, they do not specify how they accomplish that task. Our category of separation of work and personal lives may overlap with Farrenkopf's (1992) category of adopting a detached attitude. Farrenkopf found that 25% of his sample adopt a detached attitude as a way to cope. In contrast, a much smaller percentage of our respondents specify adopting a detached attitude as a coping strategy. Farrenkopf describes "attitude adjustment" involving detaching investment from outcomes of treatment as a "survival technique." Our respondents suggest that they find the need to maintain clear boundaries between professional and personal lives, but not necessarily through reducing their investment in their work or lowering expectations of treatment success.

We know that therapists who work with sex offenders 1) find their work difficult; 2) avoid discussing it with "outsiders"; 3) separate work from personal lives; and 4) consider support from other therapists in the field crucial. Our respondents are clear about the need for supervision as an essential form of support. Most respondents rely heavily on supervision as a way to address their experiences in working with offenders. Approximately one-third of the respondents seek supervision more frequently once they begin to work with sex offenders than they did when working with other client populations. Most respondents report that they receive supervision on at least a monthly or an "as-needed" basis. Given that our respondents represent experienced practitioners, the reliance on supervision and consultation may be surprising to practitioners who work with other client populations. The primary benefits that respondents attribute to supervision and consultation include either validating the therapists' perceptions or benefitting from others' perceptions, which may be the same benefits experienced by practitioners who enjoy support from other sex-offender therapists.

Many respondents enter therapy for themselves after beginning to work with offenders. Because most therapists had been working in the field for several years before beginning to work with sex offenders, this finding suggests that practitioners are affected by their work with offenders differently from work with other client populations.

Conclusion

The purpose of this exploratory study was to examine the impact on practitioners of working with sex offenders. We sought to examine a range of possible responses to working with offenders through a qualitative analysis of their thoughtful responses to open-ended questions.

This is an area that requires further exploration. In conducting the analysis of our results, many questions emerged about the possible correlations that may exist among different responses. However, we believed that confining ourselves to reporting the descriptive results at this point of inquiry was necessary. We hope to begin to examine the relationships among these categories in our next phase of investigation. For example, we are curious about the connections among gender, the perception of danger while working with this population, and the motivation to continue working with sex offenders.

References

Farrenkopf, T. (1992). *What happens to therapists who work with sex offenders?* Sex offender treatment: Psychological and medical approaches. New York: Haworth.

McCann, L., & Pearlman, L.A. (1990). Vicarious traumatization: A framework for understanding the psychological effects of working with victims. *The Journal of Traumatic Stress, 3,* 131-149.

Strasburger, L.H. (1986). The treatment of antisocial syndromes: The therapist's feelings. In W.H. Reid, D. Dorr, J.I. Walker, and J.W. Bonner (Eds.) *Unmasking the psychopath: Antisocial personality and related syndromes.* New York: Norton.

5

Vicarious Traumatization: A Preliminary Study

KATHLEEN D. RICH, Ph.D.[1]

Increasingly, the literature reports the effects on the therapist of providing psychotherapy to clients (Chessick, 1978; Coltart, 1993; Grosch & Olsen, 1994; Guy, 1987; Hellman, Morrison, & Abramowitz, 1986; Kilburg, Nathan, & Thoreson, 1986; Peterson, 1994; Rippere & Williams, 1985). Among the concepts used to describe the impact of working with clients who have suffered trauma is that of vicarious traumatization (McCann & Pearlman, 1990b), a process by which therapists treating survivors of trauma are vulnerable to alterations in their own cognitive schemata, leading to alterations in their adaptation to the world. Vicarious traumatization is not considered to be the same phenomenon as burnout, which refers to stress incurred by employees confronted with intractable situations or workers who meet with unrealistic expectations (Farber, 1983). Vicarious traumatization is also different from countertransference, which refers to previously existing personal issues evoked in the therapist when interacting with a client (Marshall & Marshall, 1988).

McCann and Pearlman (1990a) generated a self-constructivist theory of development to explore the effects of trauma on survivors. They posited a three-stage process in which life experiences influence cognitive schema, generally concerning safety, trust, power, esteem, and intimacy, leading to adaptation in emotional, cognitive, biological, behavioral, and interpersonal areas of the individual (see also McCann, Sakheim, & Abrahamson, 1988). Applying this theory to therapists working with trauma survivors (McCann & Pearlman, 1990b, 1993), they described examples of profound change in therapists' cognitive schemata and adaptations after hearing about traumatic events from their clients. "Vicarious traumatization" is the phenomenon in which the therapist becomes trauma-

[1] Kathleen Rich, Ph.D., L.C.S.W., Portland Oregon, has a clinical practice with McGovern Associates and is an adjunct faculty member in both the School of Professional Psychology at Pacific University in Forest Grove, OR, and the Counseling Psychology Graduate Program at Lewis and Clark College in Portland, OR.

tized vicariously in response to a client's account of traumatic experiences (McCann & Pearlman, 1993; Pearlman & McCann, 1993).

From this pioneering work, a framework for understanding became available. However, the types of therapists' schemata and cognitions usually affected have been only partially explored (Brett & Ostroff, 1985). Also, although theoretically applicable to professionals other than therapists and to treaters of both perpetrators and survivors of harm, the incidence of vicarious traumatization has not been well documented. To explore the potential breadth of vicarious traumatization across professions, to understand the kinds of alterations in both schemata and adaptations of those who have been vicariously traumatized, and to gain an initial understanding of the ways in which professionals were wanting and/or trying to take care of themselves, the following preliminary study was undertaken.

Method

Research Participants and Procedure

Data were collected from four separate groups of workshop and conference attenders. These attenders were given an informed consent cover letter and then volunteered to complete a questionnaire.

Group I: Group I comprises attenders at a presentation, *Vicarious Traumatization: Understanding and Transforming the Traumatization of Professionals Who Work with Survivors and Perpetrators of Violence and Victimization*, offered February 28, 1992, and sponsored by Portland University and Morrison Center in Portland, Oregon. Of attenders, 14 males and 35 females responded to the questionnaire. The average age of respondents was 38.2, with a range of 25 to 60 years of age.

Group II: Group II comprises attenders at a presentation, *Resolving the Sexual Dilemmas of Your Patients and Clients: Current Assessment and Treatment Strategies*, offered by McGovern & Associates in Portland, Oregon, on December 9, 1993. Of attenders, 4 males and 14 females completed the questionnaire. The average age of respondents was 41.6 and ranged from 31 to 62 years old.

Group III: Group III comprises attenders at a presentation, *Childhood Trauma: Dissociation and the Healing Process*, offered October 7, 1994 under the auspices of Alternatives to Sexual Abuse in Portland, Oregon. Of attenders, 12 males and 38 females completed the questionnaire. The average age of respondents was 42.1, with a range of 25 to 69 years of age.

Group IV: Group IV comprised attenders at the *Third International Conference on Sexual Exploitation by Health Professionals, Psychotherapists and Clergy*, offered October 13-15, 1994 in Toronto, Canada. Of attenders, 3 males and 15 females completed the questionnaire. The average age of respondents was 42.6 ranging from 27 to 55 years old.

Instrument

A three-part questionnaire was developed for this study. The first part collected demographic data on participants. The second part contained 58 true-false questions derived from categories of life experiences, cognitive schemata, and adaptations (see Table 1). The third part of the questionnaire consisted of open-ended questions designed to explore 1) processes participants found helpful in handling traumatic material encountered during work; 2) wishes participants had for tech-

Table 1: Questionnaire Part 2

1. My formal training prepared me well to handle the work I do.
2. I feel just as (feminine/masculine-whichever applies) as I did before starting this job.
3. I went to work in this field to try to right the traumatic wrongs in my own past.
4. I believe I suffer from vicarious traumatization.
5. I wish I had a better way to handle the stress in my life.
6. I hear individuals recount traumatic material from their lives in the course of my work.
7. I feel very safe at work.
8. I live alone.
9. I trust other people as much as I have ever trusted them since working at this job.
10. I have endured a traumatic experience while doing my present job.
11. If I know a TV program or movie is about trauma, I avoid seeing it.
12. My coworkers seem to understand and support the kind of work I do.
13. I have more bad dreams since starting this job.
14. My neighborhood has a high crime rate.
15. I am a survivor of trauma in my childhood.
16. I have not seen the world as meaningful/orderly since doing this job.
17. I have sought personal therapy since beginning this job.
18. I enjoy my sex life as much as I ever did before doing this job.
19. Since starting to work at this job, I have taken a self defense class.
20. Bad images of traumatic material I heard at work intrude on personal life.
21. I enjoy life as much as I ever did before starting this work.
22. I feel confident in my ability to make a difference in my world.
23. I am beginning to see males as more harmful since doing this work.
24. I seem to worry more about the safety of my family since I started doing this work.
25. It has been harder for me to develop close friends since I started this work.
26. Other professionals value the work I do and let me know.
27. I enjoy doing the work I do now.
28. I actively believe and practice my spiritual/religious values in my daily life.

29. When I hear about others' trauma at work I feel guilty since my own life has been relatively trauma free.
30. I find I drink more alcohol since starting this work.
31. The system as it is works well to help my clients.
32. I exercise 3 times a week.
33. I belong to a support groups where I can discuss the traumatic cases I see.
34. I tend to avoid or delay working with my more traumatic cases.
35. I am less compassionate than I was before taking this job.
36. I got a permit and learned to handle a firearm since taking this job.
37. I find it difficult not to over identify with the victim/survivor.
38. I tend to avoid going out at night by myself.
39. People have commented that I seem cynical.
40. I feel women are extremely vulnerable and are likely to be harmed.
41. I am no more easily discouraged than I ever was since taking this job.
42. My vacation time adequately lets me rest and get away from the concerns of my work.
43. I have been involved in court in the course of doing my work.
44. I find it difficult not to become enraged at perpetrators.
45. I feel proud to be an American and live in America.
46. I am more anxious since I started doing this work.
47. I feel like I have failed if the people I serve at work have been harmed.
48. Since doing this work I feel somewhat removed from my circle of family and friends.
49. I have experienced flashbacks of my client's trauma.
50. As a part of my work I must maintain confidentiality.
51. I feel isolated/alone in doing the work I do.
52. I find I feel more depressed/sad since engaging in this work.
53. Empowering survivors empowers me.
54. I believe that the work I do will make a difference in people's lives.
55. I harbor secret questions about the actions and motives of new people I meet in my personal life.
56. I feel at odds with my world.
57. I feel I have what I need to have to mange the strains of my job.
58. My professional organization is a place I can turn for support.

niques that would help them handle traumatic material encountered at work; and 3) any other comments participants wanted to make.

Data

The four groups of attenders were combined, yielding a total of 135 respondents to the questionnaire. Answers to all true-or-false questions were transformed into percentages in the indicated direction, true (T) or false (F). Question 45 was dropped from analysis because respondents came from Canada and America. Besides demographic information collected at the beginning of the questionnaire, general information also was gathered from some true-false questions (Table 2).

Table 2: General Information

Question	Percentage Responding True
6. I hear individuals recount traumatic material from their lives in the course of my work.	99
50. As part of my work I must maintain confidentiality.	99
43. I have been involved in court in the course of doing my work.	72
4. I believe I suffer from vicarious traumatization.	62
15. I am a survivor of trauma in my childhood.	52
10. I have endured a traumatic experience while doing my present job.	40
38. I tend to avoid going out at night by myself.	36
31. The system as it is works well to help my clients.	21
8. I live alone.	20
3. I went to work in this field to try to right the traumatic wrongs in my own past.	14
14. My neighborhood has a high crime rate.	13
29. When I hear about others' trauma at work I feel guilty since my own life has been relatively trauma free.	10

Responses to Question 4 ("I believe I suffer vicarious traumatization") were sorted into two groups, (T)/(F), and compared to the remaining questions, excluding the general information questions listed in Table 2. Table 3 depicts responses to those questions in which slight differences between respondents identifying themselves as vicariously traumatized (VT) and those not identifying themselves as vicariously traumatized (OVT) were observed. For purposes of data inspection, chi-square tests were conducted on raw scores, comparing VT and OVT groups to true-false answers to the remaining questions. Slight differences were identified as those showing chi-square probabilities of .100 or higher. The range of probabilities was .102 to .849. Results were reported in descending order of probabilities, with responses having highest probabilities listed first.

Table 3: Differences Between VT[2]and OVT[3]
Groups with Probabilities .100 or Higher

Answer[4]	Question	% of Total Answering in Scored Direction	% VT Answering in Scored Direction	% OVT Answering in Scored Direction
T	55	42	43.4	41.7
F	28	34	34.6	37.5
T	36	5	4.8	6.3
T	19	20	21.7	18.8
F	18	35	36.1	31.9
F	27	12	13.4	10.4
T	25	15	16.9	12.5
F	33	61	63.1	56.3
F	53	18	16	21.7
F	58	60	61.9	54.2
F	54	2	1.5	4.2
T	35	20	22.9	14.6
T	44	46	50	38.3
T	17	55	59.5	47.9
T	30	12	14.5	6.3
T	40	49	53.5	39.6
T	11	57	61.9	47.9
F	26	17	21.7	10.4

[2] VT = Vicariously traumatized
[3] OVT = Not vicariously traumatized
[4] T = True; F = False

Table 4 depicts responses to those questions in which differences between VT and OVT groups showed chi-square probabilities of .099 or lower. The range of probabilities was .000 to .094. Results were reported in ascending order of probabilities, with responses having lowest probabilities listed first.

Table 4: Differences Between VT[5] and OVT[6]
Groups with Probabilities .099 or Lower

Answer[7]	Question	% of Total Answering in Scored Direction	% VT Answering in Scored Direction	% OVT Answering in Scored Direction
T	20	56	77.4	21.3
T	5	62	80.5	37.5
T	56	27	38.1	6.3

Table 4: (*Continued*)

Answer[7]	Question	% of Total Answering in Scored Direction	% VT Answering in Scored Direction	% OVT Answering in Scored Direction
F	57	47	60.2	27.1
T	46	41	54.8	16.7
F	41	50	65.1	23.4
F	9	56	67.5	39.6
F	42	56	66.7	37.5
T	23	48	59.0	31.9
T	52	40	48.8	22.9
F	32	41	51.2	27.1
T	13	20	27.7	8.3
T	37	30	38.1	16.7
T	48	27	35.7	14.6
T	49	23	29.8	10.4
F	21	30	36.9	16.7
T	16	28	34.9	17.0
F	7	22	28.6	12.5
T	39	27	33.3	16.7
T	24	56	34.2	45.8
T	51	39	47.0	29.2
F	1	67	72.6	56.3
F	22	22	28.6	12.5
F	2	20	25.3	12.5
T	47	27	33.3	19.0
F	12	10	13.8	4.3
T	34	24	29.8	16.7

[5] VT = Vicariously traumatized
[6] OVT = Not vicariously traumatized
[7] T = True; F = False

Responses to open-ended questions were tabulated (Table 5). Several similar items were endorsed both as wanted by some participants and as used for assistance by others. A few items were wanted by some participants but not mentioned as helpful by others. Some ideas that did not appear on the desired-items list were mentioned as helpful by those self-described as not vicariously traumatized.

Results

Demographic Data

Participants in this study came from nine states (Arizona, California, Idaho, Maryland, Michigan, Nevada, Oregon, Pennsylvania, Washington) and three Canadian provinces (British Columbia, Manitoba, Ontario). The highest academic

Table 5. Answers to Open-Ended Questions

What is Wanted	What Helps
Supervision	Supervision
Supportive colleagues	Supportive colleagues
Support groups	Support groups
More time off from work	More time off from work
Personal treatment	Personal treatment
Exercise	Exercise
Active spirituality	Active spirituality
Time with friends/Friends not in profession	Time with friends/Friends not in profession
Time for family	Time for family
Set limits	Set limits
*Agency administrative support for employees handling trauma	†Hobbies
*Time to process things alone	†Spouse: supportive &/or in another field
*Massage	†Humor
*More money	†Objectivity
*More fun	†Rest/good diet/regular relaxation
	†IBelief in survivor strengths
	†Pets
	†Avoid cynicism
	†Refuse to imagine trauma scene
	†Stable past or past personal trauma worked through

*Seen as desirable but not identified by anyone as helpful.
†Endorsed by participants in OVT group.

degrees held by participants were medical degrees (3), doctorates of jurisprudence (4), doctorate degrees (34), master's degrees (65), bachelor degrees (23), and others (6). The mean job length for participants was 6.25 years, ranging from less than 1 year to more than 40 years. Fifty percent of participants stated that they served all ages; 15% served adults only; 11% served children and adolescents; 10% served adolescents only; 7% served adolescents and adults; 3% served children only; and 4% did not answer.

Participants reported hearing about trauma an average of 38% of each work day, with a range of less than 15% to 100%, a median of 40% and a mode of 50 %. In addition, 72% of respondents reported mental health facilities as their primary work settings, with 8% in state agencies (such as child protection), 6% in corrections, 5% in law, 3% in education, 2% in medicine and 4% in other work settings. The most commonly reported secondary setting was education (10%) with 22% distributed among all aforementioned professions other than mental health, and 68% did not respond.

Of the 135 participants, 86 reported encountering both perpetrators and survivors in the course of their work, 37 reported encountering only survivors, 3 reported encountering only perpetrators of harm, and 9 did not answer or encountered neither perpetrators nor survivors of harm. Furthermore, 96% of the participants answered "Yes" to hearing about both child sexual abuse and emotional abuse in the course of their work. Ninety-one percent heard about physical abuse; 83% heard about rape, 81% about child neglect, 42% about street crime, 28% about murder, 12% about war and 26% about other harm, such as professionals abusing clients. On the other hand, 89% of respondents reported some degree of satisfaction with their jobs; the other 11% described some level of dissatisfaction.

Table 2: General Information

Ninety-nine percent of respondents reported that they hear traumatic material during the day and must maintain confidentiality. Seventy-two percent were involved with the court system, and 62% reported believing they suffer from vicarious traumatization. Fifty-two percent were survivors of childhood trauma and 40% reported that they had endured a traumatic experience while in their current positions. Fourteen percent reported working in the profession to rectify traumatization in their pasts, whereas 10% identified their own lives as relatively trauma-free. Thirty-six percent reported avoiding venturing out alone at night. Twenty percent lived alone, and 13% lived in a high-crime-rate neighborhood. Only 21% believed the current system works well to help clients.

Table 3: Small Differences Between VT and OVT Groups

Forty-two percent of the combined respondents stated they harbor questions about the actions and motives of new people they meet, with barely any differences between VT and OVT groups. Similar percentages of both VT and OVT groups answered false to a question about practicing spiritual beliefs daily, with 34% of the total group responding false to this question. Five percent of the total group reported learning to handle firearms, and 20% took a self-defense class since starting their jobs. Thirty-five percent of the total group answered false to the statement that they enjoyed sex as much as ever, with only a slightly higher percentage of the VT group answering false. Twelve percent of the total group reported not enjoying the work at the time of the survey. Fifteen percent of the total respondents reported finding it harder to develop close friends since starting the work, and 61% reported that they did not belong to a support group. Eighteen percent overall stated that they did not believe empowering others empowered themselves, and 60% of respondents did not find their professional organization supportive.

Only two percent of the total group did not think the work they did makes a difference in others' lives. Twenty percent of the overall group reported believing that they were less compassionate at the time of the study than they had been when they began work, and 46% reported feeling enraged at perpetrators, with a few more of the VT than OVT group endorsing both these items. Fifty-five percent of the total group reported seeking therapy, and 12% admitted to drinking more alcohol since beginning the job, with a somewhat greater percentage of the VT group endorsing those items. Forty-nine percent of the total group reported seeing women as more vulnerable, and 57% stated that they avoid programs about trauma, with more of the VT agreeing with those items. Seventeen percent of the total group reported not feeling that their co-workers value what they do, again with a higher representation in the VT group.

Table 4: Large Differences Between VT and OVT Groups

This table shows strong differences between VT and OVT groups. The VT group reported that they wanted a better way to handle the stress in their lives, and they reported personally experiencing bad images of traumatic material they heard at work. In addition, VT group members report feeling more easily discouraged and more anxious than respondents in the OVT group, and more VT group respondents reported that they felt at odds with the world than did OVT group members. A higher percentage of VT group members reported not feeling they possess the necessary skills to manage the stress of their jobs as compared with OVT group members. Fifty-six percent of the total group reported decreased trust of others, with a much higher proportion of the VT group than the OVT expressing this change. More of the VT group than the OVT group reported that they failed to relieve stress during vacations.

More VT group members than OVT respondents reported seeing men as more harmful since beginning this work, and more reported depression than OVT group members. Far more of the VT group than OVT group reported failing to exercise three times a week. A much higher percentage of the VT group reported experiencing bad dreams of the client's traumatic material and over-identifying with the client than did the OVT group. More of the VT group than OVT group report being removed somewhat from their friends and enjoying life less. Many more VT than OVT group members reported experiencing flashbacks of their clients' traumatic material. Higher percentages of VT group members than OVT members stated that they did not see the world as orderly and did not feel safe at work. Cynicism is reported more frequently among VT respondents than among the OVT group. More of the VT than OVT group members expressed worry about their families' safety. A higher percentage of VT than OVT group members reported feeling isolated at work and ill-prepared by formal training to handle the work. Twenty-two percent of the total group responded that they did not believe their work makes a difference in their world, with greater numbers of VT than OVT members reporting this.

A higher percentage of VT than OVT members reported not feeling as masculine or feminine since they began providing abuse-related treatment. More VT than OVT respondents reported believing they had failed if the people they served had been harmed, and a higher proportion of the VT group than OVT group put off trauma cases. Only 10% of the total respondents reported that they did not think their co-workers understood or supported their work, but a higher proportion of VT than OVT group members reported feeling they were not understood or supported by co-workers.

Table 5: Answers to Open-ended Questions

Items generated by participants as both desired and helpful in handling their jobs include 1) supervision, especially clinical supervision in which case materials are debriefed; 2) support from colleagues and others; and 3) establishment of limits in their work. Personal therapy, exercise, and active practice of spirituality were mentioned as desired and helpful. Time for family and friends, especially those not in the field, were also included in lists of both "desired" and "helpful" items.

Respondents reported a wish for 1) agency or administrative support for employees handling trauma, including provision of training and supervision; 2) respect for the impact of trauma on workers; and 3) leave, through time off or re-strictions of cases. Increased time alone, massage, more money, and more fun were also reported as desirable.

Members of the OVT group mentioned the following as helpful to them: 1) hobbies, with many examples of being involved with nature; 2) involvement with pets; 3) humor; and 4) being objective. Rest, good diet and regular relaxation were also mentioned. Several OVT group members identified a supportive spouse and a spouse outside the field as helpful. Respondents reported beliefs in survivor strengths and a refusal to imagine a trauma scene to be useful. Some OVT members saw a stable personal past or having worked through past per-sonal trauma as useful as well.

Discussion

CAVEAT EMPTOR! This research is preliminary and exploratory. Inferential sta-tistics were not reported because the sample was not random. Applying general conclusions about these results to the population at large is suspect. The ques-tionnaire elicited self-report data, which are subject to distortion and difficult to verify. The questionnaire is not yet standardized, with traditional reliability and validity data yet unavailable. The above concerns limit this discussion to findings from the 135 participants who came from diverse locations and occupations.

In this study, 62% of respondents identified themselves as vicariously traumatized. When those people were differentiated from the non-vicariously traumatized participants, several themes emerged, revealing specific experiences that may relate to subsequent alterations in cognitive schemata and adaptations described earlier in various sources by McCann and Pearlman.

A much higher percentage of vicariously traumatized respondents report experiences of flashbacks, bad dreams and bad images of *clients'* traumatic mater-ial. These phenomena represent the *sine qua non* of vicarious traumatization.

Safety schemata are altered in the VT group: more of them report anxiety, worry about their families, and seeing men as more harmful than the non-vicariously traumatized group, while fewer of the traumatized report feeling safe at work. Trust schemata are affected, with a higher percentage of vicariously traumatized respondents reporting lower trust, more cynicism, and seeing the world as less orderly than the non-vicariously traumatized group reports.

Power schema findings indicate a higher percentage of vicariously traumatized participants feel depressed and easily discouraged. They report feeling like a personal failure if their clients are harmed and an inability to believe their work makes a difference in their clients' lives. Lowered perceptions of self as just as masculine or feminine as ever and reduced belief that co-workers understand or support their work reflect alteration in the esteem schemata of the vicariously traumatized group. Interestingly, 34% of the total group reports that they did not enjoy their sex lives as much as ever, with small differences between the VT and OVT groups, whereas differences between VT and OVT groups were larger concerning gender identity. This may indicate that many causes outside vicarious traumatization may influence reduced sexual enjoyment, but gender identity may be more directly affected by or more sensitive to vicarious traumatization than sexual enjoyment.

Intimacy schemata are also altered in the vicariously traumatized group. They report feeling more isolated than previously, somewhat removed from family and friends, at odds with the world, and over-identified with clients.

To adapt, the vicariously traumatized group expresses a wish for a better way to handle stress in general and strains in their jobs. More members of the VT group tend to avoid trauma cases, fewer find respite in vacations, and fewer exercise regularly than the non-vicariously traumatized respondents. Fewer feel well prepared by formal training for their work than the OVT group. More of the vicariously traumatized group also report not enjoying life as much since taking on this work.

Only small differences were noted between VT and OVT groups in several areas. Most of the total respondent sample reports enjoying their work. Esteem schemata reflect that nearly all participants in this study believe they make an impact on clients' lives, and a majority are personally empowered by empowering others. Concerning safety schemata, virtually no differences exist between VT and OVT groups but more than 40% of all participants express wariness about others' motives, possibly reflecting general trends in an increasingly violent society. Neither VT nor OVT group members found it particularly difficult to develop close friends, but nearly two-thirds of both groups combined reported not belonging to support groups and not finding support from their professional organization. A very small percentage of both groups has adapted by learning to handle firearms or taking self-defense classes.

Some of the small differences noted between VT and OVT groups showed higher in the VT groups. These differences must be regarded carefully and need further study. Results suggest the VT group's safety schemata could be affected as reflected in their reports of seeing women as more vulnerable. The VT group's esteem schemata may be affected by not feeling valued by co-workers. Concerning adaptation, more of the group report a decrease in compassion, and a tendency to become enraged at perpetrators is reported by a slightly higher number of the vicariously traumatized participants than the non-vicariously traumatized group. A higher percentage of vicariously traumatized group members adapted through personal therapy and by avoidance of movies and television programs with violent content than did OVT members. A troubling adaptation is noted in reports that 30% of the total respondents were drinking more alcohol since starting their jobs, with greater numbers of VT than OVT group members represented in this finding.

Hints from the open-ended questions point to schemata and adaptations respondents found helpful. The expression of wishes for support, through clinical supervision or from family and friends, reflects a possible shift in intimacy schema of the vicariously traumatized individuals. Physical self-care through exercise, rest, good diet and regular relaxation are biological adaptations found useful by some. Cognitive adaptations, using humor, objectivity and belief in survivor strengths are used to offset schemata of powerlessness. Personal therapy, personal time, and personal involvement in spirituality could positively influence safety, trust and esteem schemata as well. Many of these suggestions repeat suggestions in the literature for professional self-care (Medeiros & Prochaska, 1988; Munroe & Shay, 1993).

Of interest is that 89% of all participants report some degree of job satisfaction and enjoying their work, and 82% believe empowering others empowers themselves. Ninety-eight percent of the total group of respondents believe their work makes a difference in people's lives. These positive attitudes overall may not be determinants in the presence of vicarious traumatization.

Seventy-nine percent of all respondents report not thinking the system works well to help clients, and 60% report a lack of support by professional organizations. Many participants (40%) reported personally enduring trauma since starting their jobs. However, again, these negative perceptions and experiences may not be likely causal factors in the etiology of vicarious traumatization. If anything, the disruption in cognitive schemata and adaptations in the vicariously traumatized group reported in this study is manifested in desire for but absence of better ways to cope with personal and professional stresses.

The results of this preliminary and exploratory study suggest the presence of vicarious traumatization may be detected by an individual experiencing it across a variety of professions, including those serving both perpetrators and survivors of many types of trauma. Results also reveal crucial schematic areas and adaptations in which vicariously and non-vicariously traumatized individuals report differences. The participants' suggestions for help with issues of vicarious traumatization are those that may combat altered schemata and adaptations in a vicariously traumatized individual. The large percentage of individuals in the vicariously traumatized group wanting better ways to handle stress suggests they experience an entrenchment in self-harmful schemata and adaptations, most probably requiring intervention from external sources. Clinical supervision, support from others and good physical self-care were examples of intervention suggested by respondents to offset vicarious traumatization.

These initial findings may have heuristic value in generating more rigorous studies in the assessment and relief of vicarious traumatization. With heightened recognition of trauma in society, professionals in many fields will need to be aware also of the potential for vicarious traumatization and the ways to address it. As further study broadens professionals' awareness of the potential for self-harm while helping others, the impetus to find and implement effective self-care techniques for professionals is underscored, which is the intent of this preliminary look at vicarious traumatization.

References

Brett, E.A., & Ostroff, R. (1985). Imagery and posttraumatic stress disorder: An overview. *American Journal of Psychiatry, 142*(4), 417-424.

Chessick, R.D. (1978). The sad soul of the psychiatrist. *Bulletin of the Menninger Clinic, 42*(1), 1-9.

Coltart, N. (1993). *How to survive as a psychotherapist.* Northvale, NJ: Jason Aronson.

Farber, B.A. (Ed.) (1983). *Stress and burnout in the human service professions.* New York: Pergamon Press.

Grosch, W.N., & Olsen, D.C. (1994). *When helping starts to hurt: A new look at burnout among psychotherapists.* New York: Norton.

Guy, J.D. (1987). *The personal life of the psychotherapist: The impact of clinical practice on the therapist's intimate relationships and emotional well-being.* New York: Wiley.

Hellman, I.D., Morrison, T.L., & Abramowitz, S.I. (1986). The stresses of psychotherapeutic work: A replication and extension. *Journal of Clinical Psychology, 42*(1), 197-205.

Kilburg, R.R., Nathan, P.E., & Thoreson, R.W. (Eds.). (1986). *Professionals in distress: Issues, syndromes, and solutions in psychology.* Washington, D.C.: American Psychological Association, Inc.

Marshall, R.J., & Marshall, S.V. (1988). *The transference-countertransference matrix: The emotional-cognitive dialogue in psychotherapy, psychoanalysis, and supervision.* New York: Columbia University Press.

McCann, I.L., & Pearlman, L.A. (1990). *Psychological trauma and the adult survivor: Theory, therapy, and transformation.* New York: Brunner/Mazel.

McCann, I.L., & Pearlman, L.A. (1990). Vicarious traumatization: A framework for understanding the psychological effects of working with victims. *Journal of Traumatic Stress, 3* (1), 131-149.

McCann, I.L., & Pearlman, L.A. (1992). Constructivist self-development theory: A theoretical framework for assessing and treating traumatized college students. *Journal of College Health, 40*(1), 189-196.

McCann, I.L., & Pearlman, L.A. (1993). Vicarious traumatization: The emotional costs of working with survivors. *Treating Abuse Today, 3*(5), 28-31.

McCann, I.L., Pearlman, L.A., Sakheim, D.K., & Abrahamson, D.J. (1988). Assessment and treatment of the adult survivor of childhood sexual abuse within a schema framework. In S.M. Sgroi (Ed.), *Vulnerable populations: Evaluation and treatment of sexually abused children and adult survivors,* (Vol. 1, pp. 77-101). Lexington, MA: Lexington Books.

McCann, I.L., Sakheim, D.K., & Abrahamson, D.J. (1988). Trauma and victimization: A model of psychological adaptation. *The Counseling Psychologist, 16*(4), 531-594.

Medeiros, M.E., & Prochaska, J.O. (1988). Coping strategies that psychotherapists use in working with stressful clients. *Professional Psychology, 19*(1), 112-114.

Munroe, J.F., & Shay, J. (1993). Prevention of secondary trauma in therapists. *Traumatic Stress Points: News for the International Society for Traumatic Stress Studies, 7*(3), 3.

Pearlman, L.A., & McCann, I.L. (1993). Vicarious traumatization among trauma therapists: Empirical findings on self-care. *Traumatic Stress Points: News for the International Society for Traumatic Stress Studies, 7*(3), 5.

Peterson, J.A. (1994). When the therapists who have sat with shattered souls are themselves shattered. *Treating Abuse Today, 4*(2), 26-27.

Rippere, V., & Williams, R. (Eds.). (1985). *Wounded healers: Mental health workers' experiences of depression.* Chichester, England: Wiley.

6

Increasing Efficacy and Eliminating Burnout In Sex-Offender Treatment

JOSEPH GIOVANNONI, R.N., M.A., M.S., C.S.[1]

A practitioner who chooses to work with sex offenders and make a living in that line of work must constantly explore ways to make the practice successful, effective, enjoyable, and ethical. The sex- offender treatment practitioner is well aware of the stress involved in helping individuals who are resistant to change. He or she must also consider ways to reduce stress and eliminate "burnout." The specialist can begin to accomplish those goals by asking: What does each client teach me about the causes of sexual assault? What treatment approach works for me? What specific interventions work for specific clients? How can I contribute to community safety, yet maintain a therapeutic relationship? How can I best serve my client in his attempt to change his maladaptive behavior and develop socially acceptable forms of sexual expression? Finally, how can I positively influence my client to correct his thinking so that he can experience love in his life rather than fear based on a need for power and control?

I have worked with sex offenders since 1984, treating more than a thousand individuals. I have also conducted 600 psychosexual assessments during that time. Since 1989, I have been contracted by the State of Hawaii Judiciary, and the Paroling Authority. I currently conduct 14 relapse prevention groups per week in which I apply principles of relapse prevention, behavior therapy, and family therapy in treatment of offenders. I work a 14-hour day involving direct contact with sex offenders. Between 1987 and 1992, I have had 45 clients who eagerly left my practice in search of another therapist because they perceived me as punitive when I introduced the waiver of confidentiality. Between January 1992 and November 1994, only one client left my practice for that reason. I still believe that the primary role of the therapist is to promote community safety.

---

[1] Joseph Giovannoni has directed relapse prevention programs for the State of Hawaii Judiciary and Paroling Authority since 1989.

In a recent review of 400 sex offenders who received treatment from me from 1987 to 1994, eight were recidivists. Six of those individuals reoffended within the first three months of treatment, and two offenders reoffended after one year in treatment. Three of those offenders were male pedophiles, three were rapists, and two were molesters of female children. Their relapses were identified through police reports, polygraphs, family reports, and personal disclosures. Currently, 156 are still active in weekly treatment sessions, and 20 are in a maintenance program with a three- to six-month follow up.

Three years ago, I developed job-related stress, with physical ailments related to the stress. I experienced attacks from difficult clients and their attorneys. I was threatened with lawsuits by unhappy clients who were incarcerated because of disclosures I made in the interests of community safety. Almost ready to relinquish a flourishing practice, I was determined to find strategies to cope with the stress. I thought the solution was to enhance my skills and learn everything possible about sex offenders from the experts. I found this additional education to be helpful, and my findings often validated my own approach and treatment methodology with offenders. It helped me develop a flourishing practice and increased my credibility.

As client volume increased, however, additional offenders came into my practice. To cope with increasing demands, I began a routine of exercise, dietary changes, and weekly massage. Also, I increased my time off for leisure activities. It helped me to manage but it did not seem to reduce how much conflict I experienced on the job. I knew that there had to a better way. Stress management required changing my perception about offenders and about me as a person and therapist.

I will outline what I believe has helped me to increase my effectiveness and reduce stress. I do not focus on treatment intervention, but rather on the principles that therapists may use as they relate to clients and probation or parole officers. I report here about how I as a sex-offender treatment specialist became clear about my intent in sex-offender treatment. Now, as I carry out the cognitive changes I have learned, I no longer experience threats, attacks, and fear of lawsuits. Occasionally, certain clients make choices not to abide by the relapse prevention principles, but when they are terminated from treatment, they understand that I do not reject them, but rather that I honor their choice of consequences.

Therapists can only heal themselves. Too many practitioners believe that behavioral change results when the appropriate interventions are skillfully applied to specific problems. An experienced therapist is well aware that an offender can learn to say all the right things and yet secretly engage in high-risk behavior. The practitioner has to determine appropriate treatment to address this obfuscation and redefine the meaning he or she gives to the relationship with each client. In my view, the therapist would find it very helpful to view the client as a teacher rather than just a patient, a sick person, or a "pervert."

Often, clients may mirror fears that some therapists feel. For me, for example, the most difficult offenders are those who murdered their victims. I have two clients who had been released on parole after serving their minimum sentence for murder and sexual assault. I could not accept their release because I believed that a murderer should be incarcerated for life. Under my contract with the State of Hawaii, I was obliged to treat those two individuals. We all fear death and violence perpetrated against ourselves. To work effectively with those clients, I had to redefine them as separate from their behavior. I had to separate their essences from their behaviors.

Similarly, to work successfully with sex offenders over the long term, the practitioner must also redefine sex-offending behavior. Judging people by their unacceptable behavior is usual. However, we know that the offender hurts others because he hates himself and projects the attack outward (Money, 1986). John Money identified the "love map," a mental template expressed in every individual*s erotic fantasies and practices. Deprivation, neglect, and abuse lead to love-map pathology generating possible paraphilia. The individual with a paraphiliac disorder projects the image of his own vandalized love map on another. To separate the person from the behavior, I found it helpful to view sexually abusive behavior as an illusion created by the offender to relieve feelings of loneliness and powerlessness. Those who offend against others are calling out for love, although they do not know the meaning of love.

By observing the offender's reasoning closely, we see that he teaches us that his sexual deviance is caused by illogical thinking. Sex offenders, who believe in the illusion of violence, reflect self-hatred; they do not accept themselves even if they are overtly narcissistic. Feeling accepted by the therapist is essential before the client is willing to consider a new way of thinking. Clinicians' judgments often mirror their own fears and inhibit their understanding of the cause of the behavior. Working with sex offenders and murderers is not for everyone. When treating sex offenders, therapists are not running an experiment from a two-way mirror, lacking all feelings. They are dealing with real people who are in pain who have separated themselves from love. As therapists, we are vulnerable to experiencing emotional swings. We need to understand the purposes that these experiences serve for ourselves as we listen to the offenders. Therapists must create a safe environment for the sex offender to speak and render himself defenseless. I create such an environment by reminding myself that *I am the presence of love in the therapeutic situation.*

The solution I found for lowering stress was to accept that I can see things differently. In the presence of a difficult client, I find it helpful not to focus on his defensive posture or his projection of anger. What I try to achieve is a sense of calm. Simply by being aware that everything we do, including working with difficult sex offenders, is a way to achieve peace, I redefined my work with sex offenders as a vehicle to achieving a peaceful state of mind. When I perceived conflict, personal attack, or physical signs of stress, I learned to say to myself: "Right now, I choose peace, and I choose to see things differently; I will therefore relieve myself of the burden of judgment." This attitudinal change helps me to drop all misperceptions and fear I anticipate, enabling me to listen without judgment. I then facilitate the offender's ability to express his feelings and thoughts. I was amazed at the increase in frequency of disclosure from clients.

If the clinician tries to listen to an offender without judgment, it is likely that the therapist will achieve clarity about the cause of the offender's behavior. Avoiding judgment does not mean overlooking the consequences of clients' actions. It requires being willing to perceive them differently, to accept *them* but not their *behavior*. I have never met an offender in my practice who loves himself, or who genuinely felt loved. Offenders view themselves as victims, and often get stuck in the "victim stance." They project this perception onto their victims. Their thinking errors reflect a view of the victim as the enemy, or as an object of pleasure; the offender justifies the offense, believing the victim is rightly his to harm. Furthermore, I view the client's behavior as a reflection of his mind. What a man thinks, he sometimes does. This philosophy makes it easier for me to accept the offender as a person, separate from his deviant behavior.

As I witness the offender's mind when it reveals the victim stance and resistance to treatment, I repeat to myself: "I am the presence of love, and I am with this person to attain peace. I do this work because it brings me peace." Identifying myself as the presence of love means making a choice to see conflict, pain, crime, and punishment through a loving, nonjudgmental filter, rather than with fear and judgment.

This cognitive adjustment is not an easy process, but it became easier as *I made the choice* to see the world with loving eyes. Often, I would forget and lapse into my old pattern of fear and judgment. At those times, I had to *switch* back into the reality of who I am in the therapeutic setting: the presence of love. In the past, I recognized that when I experienced frustration, it was because my thoughts reflected helplessness and negative self-criticism. I discovered that when I made the choice to change my attitude so that I recognize peace as a result, I began to experience peace. This process of attaining a conscious state of peace facilitated cooperation on the offender's part.

Choosing peace also requires honoring the client's choice. I cannot control what an offender chooses to do. The offender who chooses to lie disregards the principles of relapse prevention. The offender who acts out is choosing punishment. It is not my role to rescue him. I honor his choice to cause probation or parole to be revoked. I honor his choice to face the judge again. I simply remind him of his own choice and free will. If he chooses not to comply with treatment requirements, I honor his choice to be terminated from treatment and to accept the consequences of that choice. Sex offenders need conflict. They seek conflict and a way to escape what they have already chosen, punishment. As a therapist, I bear witness to his nightmare, but I choose not to be part of it. As I consciously choose peace, I know I have an opportunity to create a peaceful atmosphere, a situation more likely to evoke a choice for peace in the offender.

While training to be a nurse, I was taught to alleviate the symptoms of pain. In my training to become a therapist, I was taught to help clients solve their own problems. During my training in sex therapy, I was taught to help others to enhance loving sexual relationships, and while learning about sex-offender treatment, I was trained to modify sexually deviant behavior and correct offenders' thinking. However, during my 13 years of higher education, I was never taught how to achieve a peaceful state of mind in the therapeutic relationship. I learned to believe that to be a good therapist, I had only to master an extensive body of scientific theory and therapeutic techniques. Certainly, the theories and techniques had validity, but knowledge alone was not an antidote for my stress and burnout. I later discovered that a new clarity of mind helped me achieve a peaceful state and redefine the meaning I gave to my work that resulted in job satisfaction. Besides cognitive choice to attain a sense of peace, the most effective way I have found to achieve clarity is to be willing to be vulnerable and share with a support group of colleagues the fears, emotional reactions, and conflict that we experience with clients.

I work closely with probation officers and parole officers because I do not see them as separate from the healing formula. Furthermore, I make it clear to my clients that my role is to educate the probation and parole officer in understanding the clients' problems, so that they can help the client make relevant choices and avoid situations that present risk. Most sex offenders make poor choices and are likely to repeat old self-defeating patterns. I encourage each offender to attempt to redefine his parole and probation officers' roles as loving professionals who set limits to facilitate offenders' success in the community, not as the administrator of punishment. Clients who choose to see them as punitive agents only reflect unresolved unconscious guilt, projections of self-judgment, and a need to mirror punishment. These individuals are the ones who find themselves being revoked from probation or parole and blame others for their predicaments.

Most probation and parole officers in the State of Hawaii have a Master's degree in mental health; they are professionals trained in the relapse prevention model. I meet with them weekly to review clients' progress, clarify care plans, and discuss compliance and high risk offenders. A sharing exchange takes place with the intent to support each client's success, and to protect the community. Within the relapse model, we expect that clients will have occasional lapses, and we encourage them to reveal their difficulties so that their care plans can be modified to include certain health promoting restrictions. Initially, most sex offenders in treatment are unlikely to cooperate when they are remanded involuntarily into treatment, unless legal sanctions are in place. The offenders who show a persistent noncompliance to treatment and consistently place themselves in high-risk situations are terminated from treatment. They may be subject to revocation of parole with confinement as a consequence, if community protection warrants it. Once terminated from treatment, an offender is allowed to continue participating in group therapy until a probation or parole officer decides his disposition, or until added restrictions are in place. He is allowed to continue attending the group so he understands that he is not being rejected and that his termination simply reflects his willful and persistent noncompliance to relapse prevention goals and objectives. Without cooperation and open communication between parole or probation officers and therapists, community safety cannot be effectively achieved.

Clients cannot heal alone. The meaning given to the therapeutic relationship by all parties, including clients, therapists, probation officers, parole officers, and significant others, is key to the client's readiness to accept interventions. Separation and secrecy among these parties increase fear in the offender's mind and enhance his need to maintain his illusions. Too often, the sex-offender treatment specialist separates himself or herself from these valuable resources. We have to reject any narcissism and any need to control treatment that we possess. I found it helpful to see myself as the teacher and student as I interact with others who are directly involved in offenders' lives. Viewing my role that way reminded me that I can only change myself. If I chose to maintain my calm, it would facilitate clarity of mind and create a comfortable atmosphere in which the client feels safe to risk vulnerability. I was amazed to find that clients were more frequently willing to waive confidentiality, reveal deviant behavior and take responsibility for their actions than before I carried out those changes in my approach.

The *Code of Ethics* of The Association for the Treatment of Sexual Abusers states that the practitioner "shall be committed to community protection and safety" (p. 1). Such a requirement by therapists can only be effectively achieved with clients who waive confidentiality among therapists, probation officers, parole officers, and, in cases of incest, children's protection service workers. This sharing of information may include the client's family, significant others, minister or other spiritual adviser, and in specific situations, employer. The primary focus is for the therapist to educate these individuals about the client's cycle of abuse, high-risk situations, and vulnerability for relapse. Ethics do not mean a breach of therapeutic techniques. Although emphasizing to the client that you do not judge him is important, he is responsible for his behavior, and you will honor his choice of confinement and punishment. The therapist cannot take responsibility for the client's destructive behavior by promising to conform to the ethic of confidentiality. By assuming personal failure because we are not able to stop the client from a relapse, therapists are trying to take such responsibility. Working closely with parole or probation officers has enriched my professional life. Helping offenders redefine their probation or parole officers as the presence of love helps them see that the officers of the law are there not as the administrators of punishment but as guardian angels who are interested in his success.

To accomplish this valuable relationship of cooperation, the therapist must reconsider traditional notions of separation between the therapist and officers of public safety. Each state should consider the value of training these officers in sex-offender treatment and creating specialized units similar to those sponsored by the State of Hawaii. Therapists must also reject any grandiose ideas that they can treat the sex offender without collaboration with law enforcement personnel. Probation and parole officers can offer effective recommendations in developing care plans. They can also be helpful in reinforcing specific homework, obtaining information from significant others, doing emergency outreach to